CHICKEN RUNS

AND

VEGETABLE PLOTS

by

CHARLOTTE POPESCU

© Charlotte Popescu 2009

Published by Cavalier Paperbacks 2009

Cavalier Paperbacks
Burnham House,
Upavon,
Wilts SN9 6DU

www.cavalierpaperbacks.co.uk

This book is sold subject to the condition that it shall not,
by way of trade or otherwise, be lent, re-sold, hired out, or
otherwise circulated without the publisher's prior consent
in any form of binding or cover other than that in which it
is published and without a similar condition including this
condition being imposed on the subsequent purchaser.

ISBN 978-1-899470-29-7

Printed and bound in Great Britain by CPI Antony Rowe
Bumper's Farm, Chippenham, Wiltshire

CONTENTS

INTRODUCTION

I have kept hens in our garden for the last 13 years and enjoy every minute of it. Hens are so like humans in many ways and all have their own individual traits and personalities. Like children, they fight and bully each other, eventually establishing a pecking order. Like many people, they enjoy the sun and have their own way of sunbathing, lying on their sides and fanning out one wing. Like us with our children, mother hens protect their chicks from all dangers. They look out for them, teaching dust bathing, foraging for food and later on how to perch and like us they either say 'right that's it you're on your own' when they are six weeks old or they hang onto their chicks for far too long. I recently had to rehome some chicks and agreed that they would be ready to go at nine weeks – what I didn't factor in was that Mother Hen was not ready to say goodbye to her brood and was devastated after they'd gone – she kept calling out for them when she found a tasty tit-bit and I felt very sorry for her – luckily she was back to normal after a few days.

We have never eaten any of our own chickens and recently I have found myself unable even to buy chicken to eat. Hens already do so much for us by producing eggs, one of the most complete foods used in our diet, and one of the cleverest natural products that can be used in so many different ways; I feel they should all be given a happy life in return.

There is definitely a trend towards growing vegetables and keeping a few hens in the garden. This is not always easy as

4

chickens love vegetables and love free ranging and foraging in gardens. However in this book I will show you how you can combine the two successfully.

During the Second World War the government famously encouraged every family in Britain to 'dig for victory' by getting rid of flowerbeds and lawns and converting all their land into vegetable plots - many people also decided to keep a few hens, eggs being such an important ingredient in many recipes. Today we appear to be doing the same - so here's to: 'No' to the paddling pools and patios; 'Yes' to chicken runs and vegetable plots.

The first section is a guide to keeping chickens, covering all aspects of chicken management and I will devote a part to frequently asked questions and things that can go wrong.

The second part looks at the vegetables, herbs, shrubs and flowers that you can cultivate without the danger of your hens eating them. I concentrate on the easiest vegetables to grow especially if you don't have much space and mention the vegetable plants that your hens will really enjoy when you have finished with them so that you achieve an excellent recycling system. I am also includeing a bit about weeds in your garden and which ones your hens will eat. There are lists of chicken-proof plants and also information on plants and vegetables that hens like to eat, which you will thus need to protect from hungry hens.

The third part is an account from my Great Aunt, May Wedderburn Cannan's memoirs which shows how she managed a smallholding keeping poultry, sheep and later pigs in the 1930s and 40s. May W. Cannan was also a published First World War poet.

5

MY TOP 10 REASONS
FOR KEEPING CHICKENS

1. We love our cats and dogs but here is a pet that actually produces something edible in return.
2. You can sell surplus eggs and buy your hens' feed with your egg money, making them self sufficient.
3. Chickens have great personalities and will add beauty and interest to your garden, parading around with their different shapes, sizes and colours.
4. If you decide to keep a few chickens you will be reducing the demand for shop-bought battery eggs and hopefully this will lead to less need for hens to be kept in cages.
5. Chickens will eat your garden pests such as slugs, snails, earwigs, grubs, beetles and add fertilizer directly to your lawn.
6. Your chickens will eat weeds such as dandelion, chickweed and dock leaves.
7. You can use the chicken poo as an activator in your compost bin.
8. Chickens are very low maintenance – they do not need to be walked, brushed or kept inside.
9. They will eat many of your leftovers and love pasta, bread and rice.
10. Your hens will endlessly amuse you and make a great talking point at dinner parties.

PART ONE
HENS AS PETS
WHAT BREEDS TO GO FOR AND WHERE TO GET THEM

First of all there are no restrictions on keeping hens in your garden but do check with your neighbours to make sure they don't mind, especially if you are thinking of keeping a cockerel! Check the deeds on your house which may have a clause forbidding poultry keeping - but don't be put off - it may no longer be relevant. Local authorites can take action if they get complaints about noisy cockerels or an increase in the rat population due to feed being left on the ground. Don't worry about DEFRA - you only need to register a flock of more than 50 hens!

The most difficult decisions about keeping hens are what breeds to choose, how many, how big and what colour. Nearly every breed of large fowl has been created in a smaller version, known as miniature fowl or bantams. Bantams are smaller than hens and will eat less but will lay smaller eggs. However if you are limited on space these are definitely an option to consider.

There are a lot of hybrid hens on the market with different trade names. These have been developed by crossing breeds to develop a hen that will primarily lay more eggs in one year that a traditional pure breed would. They are also being bred to look attractive in your garden. However these hybrids won't lay so many eggs after their first two years and in that sense they are not unlike battery hens. The other disadvantage to the hybrids is that although cockerels are available for those who really want them, they don't breed true so you cannot reproduce the hybrids yourself. The Black Rock hybrids are bred by a sole breeder in Scotland and only his agents sell hens to the public.

Cross breeds, which can be a mixture of all sorts of breeds, tend to be the hardiest, live the longest and keep laying the longest, even if erratically. Cross breeds are also the easiest hens to name. If you buy hybrids or pure breeds of one type you give them names but will have real problems telling them apart as they will all look the same. People often want to know which breeds are tame and most suitable for the garden and which breeds lay the most eggs. However, quite a lot depends on the strains within a breed. For example, I have had letters from people about their tame Leghorns which traditionally are liable to be nervous and flighty.

Flighty behaviour can very much depend on management – if you spend time with your hens, feeding them, watching them and handling them, they are likely to become quite tame.

Every bird has its own individual personality, regardless of its breed. As a general rule lightweight breeds that lay white eggs are more skittish than heavy breeds that lay brown eggs. If you want dark brown eggs from the traditional breeds you should go for Maranses, Welsummers or Barnevelders. If you want pretty bantams go for gold, silver or blue-laced Wyandottes. If you want pretty bantams which are also reliable egg layers go for Sussexes. If you want small cuddly bantams suitable for young children to handle, go for Pekins (the ones with the feathery legs) but they go broody rather frequently. If you want really good broodies go for Silkies – these are covered in fine silky fluff rather than feathers – they are fantastic surrogate mothers and will take on another hen's chicks or sit and hatch duckling eggs or any other fertile eggs. If you want blue/turquoise eggs go for Araucanas from South America or the breed that has been developed from the Araucana, known as Cream Legbar. If your main priority is to get eggs every day, go for a hybrid such as Black Rock or Bovans Nera. If you want to give your hens names, don't buy four hens of exactly the same breed and colour or you will have problems distinguishing them.

If you can, try to buy at least two of any one breed as chickens seem to be happier hanging out with a friend of the same breed.

The alternative to pure breeds or hybrids is to rescue some ex-battery hens. This can be tricky if you are a first timer since they are going to need special treatment to start with. You will have to take into account that they know nothing of the outdoors, having been kept in a tiny cage throughout their lives. They will be unfit, unable to fly up on to a perch or into a nest box. You will need to give them a good sized henhouse and run and keep them confined for the first couple of weeks so that they can build up some strength and get used to their very different surroundings – they will gradually learn to scratch and have dust baths. Due to the very warm conditions in the battery unit, battery hens tend to have large floppy combs – they act as heat dissipaters – these combs will shrink in the new weather conditions as they will need to lose less heat.

You will need to keep an eye on them if it's raining – they won't be used to wet weather and you may have to encourage them to take shelter rather than stand around in the rain. You will also find your battery hens are likely to have been debeaked – the top beak is cut so that the bottom beak looks rather strange, sticking out. Do not try and cut the bottom beak – it should gradually wear down to a natural size and shape as the hen learns to free range. Debeaking is actually quite a cruel practice – hens use the tips of their beaks to manipulate and investigate as they don't have hands! The tip is also very sensitive. It is advised that you start battery hens on layers mash because that is what they are used to. Layers pellets are the same product but in a pellet form – however your new battery hens won't recognise these to start with. By all means give them corn and or/pellets after a couple of weeks. If you are not a first timer and already have a cockerel keep your ex-battery hens separate from him for at least two weeks – they've never seen a cockerel and he might do them some damage jumping on them before they are fully fit. Once your new hens have regained some feathers and built up strength and confidence they won't look back.

On the egg-laying front your rescued hens will probably only lay at about 50% production rate and certainly to start with they may drop an egg anywhere as they walk around – they will not realise they need to find a nest box. The other problem a lot of people encounter is the eggs may be misshapen or soft shelled (see pages 29 and 70) but you may be lucky and these problem eggs may not last once the hens adapt to their new surroundings. Rubber or china eggs can be useful to encourage them to lay in the nest boxes. One factor that you will need to take into account is that your ex-battery hens will probably stop laying completely a year or so after you have adopted them which will not be ideal if you were hoping for years of egg laying. The other downside to ex-battery hens is that they may be more prone to illness because they have been so intensively produced to lay a lot of eggs in as short a time as possible that their egg production systems may wear out. They could suffer from egg peritonitis where an egg can get stuck in the system and this can prove fatal.

On the upside, many people seem to be taking on ex-battery hens and recommend them highly, particularly relishing the idea of giving these poor hens a new home, loving them and finding them very friendly, amusing and rewarding to watch as they blossom and take advantage of their second chance at life. Ex-batteries recover amazingly quickly, grow new feathers and if you give them the chance to free range this will enhance the quality of their eggs hugely in a very short space of time. Later on once the egg production slows at least you can take heart in the fact that you are giving them a happy retirement and enjoy them for their different personalities and charisma and hopefully they will continue to bring smiles to your face. For ex-battery hens you need to contact the Battery Hen Welfare Trust (BHWT) and find your local contact.

The next big question is where to get your hens. One place you shouldn't go, especially if you are a beginner, is your local market – no one sends their best hens to market and you won't know how old the hens you are bidding for are or if they have problems.

You may also bid for some young looking chickens which turn out to be cockerels – I heard about a beginner who bought some at a poultry auction which turned out to be: three cockerels - they were too young for an amateur to know the difference between pullets and cockerels; a pair of silkies - they looked nice, he said, but didn't realise that a pair includes a cockerel; one silver Sussex cockerel, which he also thought was a hen !! So he ended up with five cockerels and one hen.

If you would like hybrids you can find various companies through a search on the internet that advertise Point of Lay hybrid hens. Meadowsweet Poultry have agents across the country selling hybrids. Another excellent hybrid, the Black Rock is also sold through agents. If you get hold of a copy of Country Smallholding Magazine they have an excellent Breeders' directory at the back, listing those who deal in pure breeds. Practical Poultry Magazine also has a Breeders' Directory and operate an excellent Forum on line so that you can ask others questions about your new hens as they arise. More about hybrids later.

HOUSING, SPACE AND NATURAL INCLINATIONS

The most important thing for the hens that you are going to keep is space – the more space and the more grassy areas you can give up to your hens the better for them and the happier they will be. Your eggs will also taste all the more delicious and have lovely yellow yolks. You will need to prepare their accommodation. You should have a secure hen house, preferably made of wood, which must be waterproof with perches and nest boxes. If you are a DIY enthusiast or know someone who is, you should be able to construct one. You need to make sure the roof is waterproof. Roofing felt is no longer thought a good option as red mite in particular can easily live hidden under the felt and it is more difficult to get rid of them. The roof could be made of onduline or plain treated slatted wood. The walls need to be weatherproof and the hen house does need to be well-ventilated because hens excrete half their daily amount while roosting/sleeping. You could of course adapt a garden shed, as long as you provide ventilation, perches and nest boxes.

If you decide to buy a hen house there are specialist catalogues featuring poultry houses. Particularly good examples are produced by Forsham Cottage Arks and the Domestic Fowl Trust. Always go for the biggest hen house you can afford to fit in your garden. You will almost certainly want more chickens as time goes by. If you prefer a modern alternative then you can get an Eglu from Omlet which is a cleverly designed plastic house; they also now produce a bigger version called an Eglucube. See www.omlet.co.uk

Perches are essential for roosting and should be 60 – 90cm, 2 – 3ft above the floor. If possible, perches should be wooden slats, about 5cm, 2½in wide. For bedding on the floor of the house you can use shavings (preferably first grade shavings with the dust extracted), or straw. Some people also use shredded paper.

Each laying bantam will require access to a nest box 30 – 37cm, 12 – 15in but larger birds will need 37 – 45cm, 15 – 18in of space. Once your hens have decided where to lay they will regularly queue up for the spot and have, when desperate, been known to sit on top of each other in the same nest box! Nest boxes should be placed in the darkest, cosiest corner of the hen house and filled with hay or straw. If you have several hens it is a good idea to have at least two nesting boxes.

You should by now have found out whether there are foxes in your area because this will affect what sort of housing and run you decide to use. At the same time you need to be thinking about how free range your hens are going to be. You may want to keep them entirely enclosed or may have to if you live in an urban area and don't have a large garden. In this case Arks are a good option since they are usually on wheels and can be moved to fresh patches of grass. On the other hand you may want a hen house placed in an enclosed run or yard, in which case you need to think about fencing and whether you want to pay the extra expense to make it completely fox-proof. To give you a general idea, fox-proof fencing needs to be at least 2m, 6ft high with an overhang at the top to prevent the fox climbing over it, and needs to be dug into the ground to a depth of at least 30cm, 1ft to prevent the fox digging under it. To be effective against foxes you need to buy chain link fencing as a determined fox will bite through ordinary chicken wire.

The other option is electric fencing – this will keep your hens enclosed and safe from foxes and the advantage to this is that you can move the fencing to new patches of grass. The best type is a Flexinet green electric netting – it is popular because it blends into the background. The electric net is essentially a very secure mesh made up of electrifiable polywires that will give a shock to any animal trying to get through. The spacings between the horizontal wires start off at 5cm, 2in increments for the first 4 spacings and increase thereafter making the nets suitable for bantam sized birds and above. The electric poultry netting is 105cm, 3ft 6in high and contains 12 electroplastic twines with 11 being conductors. These nets are ideal for free range chickens and come with 15 single posts and the roll is 50m, 150ft long. This form of fencing will set you back somewhere in the region of £70. You will also need a fencer unit (energiser) which could cost you around £100. Naturally you may not want to go down this route if you have small children or other family pets.

If you do not have foxes in your area, a less expensive option would be to use black plastic fruit netting around your run and to lock your hens into a secure hen house each night. The netting should keep your hens in and away from your vegetable garden if that is your aim.

If you have a large garden or field and want your hens to be completely free range you need only a secure hen house in which to close them up every evening and let them out every morning. If you do have a large garden and allow your hens to roam freely you will have very happy hens and you will be giving them the perfect existence and one that they deserve in exchange for laying you their perfect eggs.

If you grow vegetables, salads, etc, you should be warned that hens can very quickly ruin a vegetable patch. They particularly like spinach and all forms of lettuce – if you are going to give them the run of the garden you'll need to net susceptible vegetables (more of this later). However, your hens can be a useful addition to the garden – they are very good at breaking up the soil after you have dug over your vegetable garden in the winter; they forage for pests and produce droppings, which are one of the best fertilisers you can get. My bantams love following me around when I am digging the vegetable garden and are practically under my fork as I turn the soil and they grab the worms. You should also allocate, if you can, a patch of bare earth where your hens can enjoy their dust baths (more of that later).

If you want to prevent your hens flying out of a run or garden then you may want to clip their wings. You need to cut back the primary feathers on one wing only so that the hen will be unbalanced and unable to fly. You must not cut too near the quills as this may make her bleed. As a general rule you need to clip the first three or four flight feathers back to half length. On heavy breeds this should prevent them getting more than a few inches off the ground but the lighter breeds will still be able to fly up to 2m, 6ft even with one wing clipped.

I must admit that my hens – I have over 30 – are completely free range and I let those that want to roost in the trees, do so. This is perfectly natural behaviour for them, following the example of their red jungle fowl ancestors. Many of them go high up in a conifer tree, safe from predators. Those that go up in the tree do tend to be the lighter breeds and the cross breeds. On the whole the hybrids prefer going in the hutches as do the Pekins.

FEEDING

A normal sized hen needs about 100g, 4oz of food a day in the form of grain. This is a rough guide - hens like to eat small quantities throughout the day so food must be available to them at all times. Feed can be supplied as mixed poultry grain, layers pellets or layers mash. Mixed grain consists of wheat, barley, oats and maize. Pellets and mash consist of ground poultry grain with various other ingredients added, including soya, essential fatty acids and methionine, an amino acid. Calcium and phosphorus are added which help towards strong egg shells plus vitaimns and trace elements. These pellets can also contain pigments lutein and zeaxthin from marigold and maize extracts and citranaxanthin naturally found in fruits which help the yolk colour. But both meat and bone meal were withdrawn from animal feed in 1996. Pellets are small and cylindrical – they are clean and easy for hens to eat but if confined the hens can get bored. Mash, on the other hand, keeps the birds busy for hours because it is harder to pick up and can be fed dry or wet. The main problems with layers mash is that some of it can go to waste. For chicks the grains are ground down to form crumbs. Chick crumbs also contain a coccidiostat, an anti-parasite drug that is intended to prevent intestinal disease caused by a single-celled parasite named coccidia.

Between eight and eighteen weeks teenage chicks can be fed on growers' pellets. Don't start pullets on layers pellets too early - you don't want them starting to lay eggs too early in their lives as prolapse may occur (this is where some of the hen's insides come out through the vent and need to be pushed back in). It is advisable to start pullets on a low protein diet of wheat to avoid early maturity. Thereafter, if your hens are confined, layers pellets are a good option because they contain everything the hens need in their diet. Some people feed layers pellets in the morning and mixed grains in the evening.

Layers pellets are often recommended because they are formulated to be a scientifically balanced diet and giving treats and kitchen scraps will unbalance this diet. This is because your hens may fill up on kitchen scraps which do not have all the proteins, vitamins and minerals that are found in layers pellets. However for free ranging hens, I am in favour of a more varied diet – like us, I think they thrive on a variety of foods. Hens are omnivores; our domestic hens are all descended from the red jungle fowl who would have survived on all the food available in a forest which would have included grains, green stuff, berries, insects and grubs and even small animals such as mice.

It is no longer legal to feed kitchen scraps to hens, because of the risk to domestic animals from contaminated meat (infections such as the Foot and Mouth Disease virus can be spread by infected meat). Fruit and veg can be fed to poultry provided strict separation procedures to avoid contact with meat are in place.

People feed layers pellets because they believe this increases egg production. My hens have lived on mixed poultry corn all their lives and I have never had a problem with lack of eggs. Since my hens are free range they forage during the day, eating insects including worms, grubs and slugs, grass and other green stuff. They also love snails and would eat frogs and small mice without hesitation. I feed them various treats such as plain cooked pasta (which they love), rice, bread, bits of pastry, cooked potatoes and vegetables and lettuce leaves. Most hens also enjoy bananas and fruit with pips, tomatoes, sunflower seeds, and bits of hard cheese. Kitchen scraps to avoid are anything salty, banana skins, uncooked potato peelings, chocolate, meat and fish. In the past I have found my hens particularly liked bacon rind. Also some hens like cucumber but this should be peeled because the skin is not good for them; don't give them avocados either which are apparently toxic to hens. They don't tend to like leeks or cooked carrots. More on vegetables and what hens like to eat will be explored later. Controversially most poultry books say do not feed chickens citrus fruits. However given in moderation, if your hens are partial to them, they will do no harm – I have heard people say their chickens rather like oranges and satsumas. What is evident is that citrus pulp contains substances at levels which can reduce overall growth and reach toxic levels for poultry – large amounts could inhibit calcium which might reduce laying abilities.

Your chickens may well benefit from apple cider vinegar which can be added to drinking water – just a quarter of a teaspoon in the drinker will be sufficient. The vinegar acts as an all round health tonic. It aids digestion, keeps the gut healthy, helps discourage worms and keeps the feathers in good condition.

I buy mixed poultry grain from a local feed merchant – this contains maize which always disappears first from the feed containers. It is the maize, along with grass and other greens which free rangers graze upon, which produces the yellow pigment found in egg yolks. I leave it to my hens to balance their own diets by taking what they want from the food hoppers and from eating wild food. This seems to work perfectly well. Some poultry experts regard maize as very fattening but if your birds are free ranging and active all day this should not affect them.

Feeders come in many sizes and are usually either plastic or galvanised steel. Plastic feeders are much cheaper and you can get them with hats to keep the food dry – however they will not last for ever. Galvanised feeders have a rain cover, will last for ever, are more sturdy and are unlikely to be knocked over. These are best slightly raised off the ground to keep the food clean – our main feeder rests on two or three bricks.

Hens producing eggs on a regular basis also need calcium in their diet. If you live on chalky soil they may be able to pick up enough from the soil, as mine do. But if you notice the shells on their eggs are particularly thin you should supplement their diet with extra calcium. You will need to buy oyster shells from your local feed merchant, or you could use your own egg shells but you should bake them first and then crush them, to avoid your hens getting a taste for fresh egg shells (which might lead to egg eating). Hens also need grit, which helps them digest food in their crop, and they can pick this up from the soil. If confined, you will need to buy grit and provide this for them. There is now a product with oyster shell and mixed grit combined. Hens and bantams also need fresh water at all times. You do not need to put water in the hens' sleeping quarters, though, as they do not need it during the night. A clove of garlic in the drinking water is said to be a good tonic for hens (but the garlic can be unexpectedly eaten by greedy hens! And then you may get garlic-tasting eggs). Some people also add a little cod liver oil either to the feed or to the water once a week. Cod liver oil is rich in vitamins A and D, omega and linoleic acid and allegedly improves feather quality and eggs! If possible drinking vessels should be put in the shade – this lessens the build-up of green algae in the containers which can be quite difficult to clean off. Special drinking containers can be bought from suppliers, as can automatic feeders which release more grain from an inner container as the hens eat it. It is advisable to keep your grain in dustbins with lids to deter vermin such as rats and mice.

It is certainly true that the more access your hens have to grass and green stuff the darker yellow the egg yolks. If your hens are confined without access to grass, then they need as much green stuff as possible. It is a good idea to hang up a cabbage (some say too much cabbage gives hens runny poos) or other green vegetables such as broccoli by a length of cord so that they are off the ground. Hens can then pick at it more easily than if left on the ground. You can give your hens fresh or dried grass clippings or weeds such as chickweed (more of that later).

Just for interest, there is over the page a table of food suitable for chickens which was issued by the Ministry of Agriculture in the 1920s. See also what my Great Aunt fed her chickens during the 1930s and 40s on her smallholding (pages 105 - 125).

Food for Pens of Ten Fowls (averaging about 6 lbs. each in weight) from the Commencement of the Laying Season.

	Weight of Food. Ounces.	Morning. Food-stuff.	Midday. Weight of Food. Ounces.	Grain.	Evening. Weight of Food. Ounces.	Grain.
I.	2	Lean meat	12	Barley	15	Wheat
	*3	Bran				
	*3	Cut clover hay				
	2	Barley meal				
II.	2	Cut raw bone	12	Oats	15	Maize
	*3	Bran				
	3	Chopped cabbage				
	2	Sharps (middling)				
III.	*2	Meat meal	12	Oats	15	Wheat
	*3	Bran				
	3	Chopped cabbage				
	2	Boiled potatoes				
IV.	2	Lean meat	12	Oats	15	Maize
	*3	Cut hay chaff				
	*3	Bran				
	2	Pea or bean meal				
V.	*3	Bran	10	Barley	15	Maize
	3	Chopped cabbage				
	4	Rough oatmeal				
	2	Lean meat				
VI.	*2	Bran	10	Oats	15	Maize
	3	Barley meal				
	4	Fine ground oats				
	*3	Cut hay chaff				

Those marked thus (*) should be scalded.

Digestive System

Chickens do not have teeth so that anything they eat goes down their throat whole and into the crop. The crop acts as a storehouse for the gizzard, which is a sort of bag in the digestive system. When the gizzard is empty, food will move down from the crop and small amounts of grit in the gizzard will help to grind the food. A hen's crop should be full at the end of the day - if you can pick your hens up, then you can make sure they are getting the right amount of food; put your fingers on her crop, it should feel nice and plump about as round as a dessertspoon. If it is almost empty then it means the hen is either being bullied and not getting her fair share of food or she is unwell.

THEIR NEEDS,
PERSONALITIES AND BEHAVIOUR

Hens have many needs - this is why it is so terrible that a huge amount of hens are still kept in battery cages. Hens, apart from making nests, laying eggs, mating with cockerels and mothering broods of chicks, love to exercise, flap their wings, preen, dust-bathe, sun-bathe, scratch, peck and forage for food and perch during the day.

In the summer when there is plenty of light, a hen's day will start at sunrise with feeding and probably egg laying. There follows a period during which hens will preen their feathers and clean the more inaccessible parts of their bodies with their beaks. The feathers are also oiled by the beak. Oil is picked up from the preen gland on the tail and distributed on the feathers. My bantams tend to do this standing on top of their various hutches, especially in winter when the grass is wet. If you can, provide somewhere for them to perch during the day either on a low fence, low branch or as I say on top of a hutch.

At about midday hens often like to relax in a dust-bath and doze in a cool place if it is hot or in the sunshine (a form of sun-bathing!) – they lie on one side and spread out their uppermost wing – they look quite strange but don't be alarmed – it is quite normal. Later on, a second peak of activity occurs in which the cockerel (if you have one) may be mating with his hens and, if not confined, all your hens will be out and about foraging for interesting food. They will also want to fill up their crops ready for the night. Hens like to sleep in groups on a perch in their houses or, like some of mine, roost up in a tree for the night. Pecking order is evident at this time because the hens who come first in the pecking order will want to sleep on the highest perches. Once they are settled on their perches, hens will retract their necks, shut their eyes, put their heads under a wing and go to sleep.

Pecking order

If you have a group of hens with a cockerel then he will be at the top of the pecking order. Hens under him will fight to be the second most powerful by pecking each other. If a hen loses a fight she will adopt a subservient pose, with her body lowered and legs bent. Incidentally, the larger a hen's comb is, the more she will be feared by others and she will probably automatically gain second place in the pecking order. If there is no cockerel in the group, the hen with the largest comb will probably be boss and will take on a male role – she may even crow! New hens introduced to an established group may take a while to achieve a pecking order – on the whole older hens will be more self-confident and expect a high rank while younger, more timid hens may go straight to the bottom of the pecking order. If you have two cocks, one will become dominant, or you may find they fight, especially if they are enclosed and you may have to separate them. If you introduce new hens to an established flock you should isolate them for the first few days to avoid bullying problems. It must also be said here that often hens and bantams develop friendships just like humans - sometimes two or three hens will stick together during the day and at night.

Dust Baths

If your hens are confined, it is important that you make up a dust bath for them. Use a large box and half fill it with dry earth, sand or ashes. Hens like to squat down and shake themselves with movements of the body and wings so that their feathers get covered in dust. The dust trickles through their feathers and onto their skin. In this way they clean themselves and the dust helps remove many of the parasites such as lice which infest the skin. Once finished, hens will give their feathers a good shake and probably go back to searching for food.

Moulting

The natural moulting time is late summer or early autumn. Most hens will stop laying then and cockerels will stop mating. Occasionally a hen will go on laying while moulting and a few may resume laying while moulting is still in progress. Moulting usually lasts between eight and 12 weeks. Feathers are lost from the head, neck, breast and body and lastly from the wings and tail. Hens born in the spring and summer will not usually moult until the autumn of the next year. Usually it is the poor egg layers that moult early and the better the layer, the later in the year she will moult.

EGGS AND EGG LAYING

Firstly eggs can have a variety of different coloured egg shells. Traditionally white shelled eggs are produced by hens with white feathers and white earlobes and brown eggs by hens with brown feathers and red earlobes. There are now exceptions because some white feathered hybrids lay brown eggs. There are also the turquoise eggs laid by Araucanas and Araucana based hybrids such as Cream Legbars which mostly have white earlobes.

Chicks born in early spring, known as pullets until they are a year old, will start to lay, with luck, in November and certainly before Christmas. Chicks that are born later in June or July will probably not start laying until January or February. Eggs from a newly-laying pullet will be small in comparison to the size that she will lay when fully grown.

An easy pointer to a hen that is laying is a red comb which is warm to the touch. Laying hens with also have erect tails. On a more technical basis, your can pick her up and feel for her pelvic bones which should be about 5cm, 2in or the width of three fingers apart. You can also test the distance between the end of the breastbone and the pelvic bones – if she is laying, there should be a width of four fingers. When she stops laying, her comb will be pale and the vent (the opening between the pelvic bones) will close to one finger's width.

Beak pigment in certain breeds can also help tell you if a hen is laying. Breeds such as Leghorns, Wyandottes and Rhode Island Reds have yellow pigment in their skin, legs and beak called xanthophylls. At the beginning of the laying period this pigment will be seen in the beak and legs. As the hen begins to lay, the pigment which is obtained from such food as yellow maize and green plants will now be required for the yolks. The pigment in the beak which starts at the base when she is not laying will move up the beak and will be seen as a ring of pigment in the middle of her beak when she is laying. It will then reach the tip of her beak, and will gradually fade away as she continues to lay. When the pigment reappears at the base of the beak this means she has stopped laying.

The yolk of the egg is formed in the ovary and is then released to travel down the oviduct. In the longest part of the oviduct much of the albumen is added and also the cord-like chalazae which keep the yolk in place. The egg is driven down by peristaltic squeezing movements to the isthmus where it receives the shell membrane. It then moves to the uterus (shell gland) where it stays for about 20 hours while the shell-forming glands get to work. More albumen is added here and calcium is released as the main constituent of the shell. The shape and colour of the shell are also determined in the uterus. Finally the bloom or cuticle is added and the egg is laid. In all, the egg has taken about 25 hours to form from ovulation to laying. The hen will stand to lay her egg – it is quite fascinating to watch this process if you happen to be there at the right time.

In a regularly laying bird, an egg is laid about every 25 to 26 hours. So within an hour of one egg being laid the process starts again. In winter the time between eggs increases so eggs are laid about every 27 to 28 hours. A hen will, in a natural state, lay 20 or so eggs – this is called a 'clutch' – and then she will have a 'pause' lasting several days and if she doesn't go broody will start laying another clutch of eggs. Hens usually have some time off laying while they are moulting in winter and will start laying again in January or February but probably only lay about half of what they manage to lay at their peak in April or May as the days lengthen. In August and September, hens will reduce the amount of eggs they are laying as the days shorten and then stop completely when they come in to moult. Hybrids will come back into lay after their moult for the winter months.

Light plays a vital role in egg production. It affects a small organ behind the eye which in turn sends messages to the ovary and affects the ovulation process. So it is natural for a hen to lay in the spring and go out of lay in the shorter days of autumn. Professional eggs farmers overcome this problem by using artificial light and are therefore able to maintain the same amount of light every day which evens out the egg production.

You may find that your pullets or indeed two or three-year-old hens are reluctant to start laying in February. This is when you can start using layers mash or pellets. It is best to feed layers mash in the morning and grain in the afternoon, otherwise they gorge themselves in the morning on grain which is full of starch and may become fat.

EGG PROBLEMS

Egg Bound

If your hen seems to be constantly going to the nest box but laying no eggs and shows signs of distress, it may be assumed that she is egg bound. The egg may be too large and will have got stuck, even though it is ready to be laid. You could try holding the bottom half of your afflicted hen over steaming water for several minutes. But do not hold her too close to the steam and make sure she is calm. This treatment generally relaxes and softens that part of the body, and the egg should be released. If the egg breaks inside the hen it will probably kill her but she will also die if she cannot pass the egg. You could also try the old fashioned cure of pouring a spoonful of olive oil or cod liver oil down your hen's throat or lubricate her vent with a little oil.

Shell-less Eggs

Soft-shelled or shell-less eggs with just the membrane around the egg can be quite a common problem especially with hybrids. This may happen in young pullets - the egg goes down through the oviduct so quickly that there is no time for the shell to be made. Sometimes the pullets are adjusting to their new egg-laying functions and the first few eggs will have no shell, but after a couple of weeks the eggs should be normal. If the egg has a very thin shell, your hen may not be getting enough calcium or vitamin D in her diet and you could try giving her crushed oyster shells and some cod liver oil in her feed. If your hen is still laying soft-shelled eggs after two or three weeks, it may be due to some inherent weakness in the strain which does not allow proper assimilation of calcium or an inherent malfunctioning of the reproductive tract - this could have been caused by infectious bronchitis or another disease when the hen was younger or intensive breeding may have led to malformed ovaries; in this case you may just decide to keep her as a pet.

Egg Eating

Shell-less eggs or eggs with thin shells in the nest box on a regular basis could lead to the vice of egg-eating. Once hens start eating eggs it can become a habit difficult to cure. One remedy would be to make the nest boxes as dark as possible and to collect your eggs more frequently. Also if you put lots of straw or hay in the nest boxes and a false egg there is a good chance the real egg will get buried as it is laid so that the guilty hen fails to find it and maybe takes a peck at the fake egg.

Egg Peritonitis (internal laying)

Egg yolks drop into the body cavity, instead of entering the oviduct. This could happen if the bird is stressed at ovulation. Mostly the yolk will be scavenged by the body defences and the hen might survive. But sometimes several may descend together or infection sets in and the resulting peritonitis can quickly become fatal. The bird will have a swollen abdomen and be lethargic and depressed. She may waddle like a duck. Unfortunately there is not a lot you can do for her.

Blood and Meat Spots and Rings

You may see a small blood spot or ring at the edge of the yolk or a meat spot in the white when you break one of your hens' eggs. These are completely harmless. When the yolk is ready it is normally released from the only area of the yolk sac that is free of blood vessels. Occasionally there is a rupture of a blood vessel in the ovary which may have occurred due to a sudden fright or possibly due to lack of vitamin A. As the egg ages the blood spot becomes paler so a bright blood spot is a sign that the egg is fresh. Meat spots appear as brown or sometimes white spots in an egg near the yolk - this may be a bit of reproductive tissue.

INTERESTING FACTS ABOUT EGGS

The Egg and its Nutritional Value

The egg is one of the most complete, nutritious and versatile foods that there is. It has a concentrated amount of protein and contains A, B C and E vitamins along with iron, phosphorus and zinc. Eggs are also a source of vitamin D which is involved with the absorption of calcium and phosphorus and necessary for bone health. Eggs are a great source of choline which is not an essential nutrient but has recently been thought to have a role in brain function. It is low in saturated fat and calories so a healthy fast food.

A report in the Daily Mail recently said that eating two eggs a day could help cut cholesterol levels. Research suggests that eggs make a nutritional contribution to those on a healthy diet. Although eggs are cholesterol-rich foods it is the saturated fats in cakes and processed meats that are more responsible for raising blood cholesterol.

Research shows that on average each person eats 2.7 eggs a week which is a surprisingly small amount.

Research has been done on eggs from hens free ranging on grass as opposed to battery eggs. Free range eggs contain more Omega-3-fatty acids. They also have less saturated fat

31

and more vitamins A, E and B12 as well as a higher percentage of folic acid.

Egg Records

The number of eggs laid by one bird in one year is 361.

The number of yolks found in one egg is apparently nine.

The biggest egg ever laid weighed is at 1lb or 450g – it had a double yolk and a double shell.

More Down to Earth Facts

There is not that much of a relation between the size of chicken and size of egg – Brahmas and Orpingtons are two of the largest breeds but lay small eggs. Appenzellers (a German breed) lay quite large eggs considering their size. As hens grow older they tend to lay larger eggs.

Eggs should always be stored large end uppermost to keep the air cell in place and the yolk in the centre.

Hard boiled eggs peel more easily if a week or two old.

Can't remember if an egg is fresh or hard boiled? Just spin the egg. If it wobbles, it's raw. If it spins easily, it's hard boiled.

A fresh egg will sink in water, a stale one will float.

Meringues are best made with egg whites from eggs that are a few days old.

Eggs contain the highest quality protein you can get. The protein in the egg is just the right mix of essential amino acids needed by humans to build tissues. Eggs also have essential vitamins and minerals. Egg yolks naturally contain vitamin D.

Fascinating Facts and Folklore

French brides break an egg on the threshold for luck and healthy babies.

There is a quaint superstitious belief, usually attributed to the Chinese, that you can stand a raw egg on end during the vernal equinox (20 March). This derives from the idea that due to the sun's equidistant position between the poles of the earth on the first day of spring special gravitational forces apply.

Coloured eggs were the universal Easter gift. Eggs were boiled and coloured with tied ribbons, onion skins, herbs and the yellow flowers of gorse and broom.

An odd number of eggs should be set under a hen (I always thought this was because they fitted together more easily under the hen). Housewives passed a lighted candle over, or pencilled crosses on the eggs to save them from foxes and weasels.

Eggs should not be set under a hen on a Sunday or in May, the month of witchcraft.

33

Spring flowers affected hatching – each primrose represented a yellow chick so a large bunch of primroses was fine but if a single primrose came into the house it would cause the hens, by imitative magic, to only hatch one egg.

'Whistling maid and crowing hen is neither good for God nor men'.

Some Egg Proverbs

Don't teach your grandmother to suck eggs – a caution against offering advice to the wise.

You cannot make an omelette without breaking eggs.

Don't put all your eggs in one basket – don't chance everything on a single venture.

He that would have eggs, must endure the clucking of the hen.

I have other eggs to fry.

Egg Sayings

An egg is only an egg's way of making another egg. *Samuel Butler*

THE EGGS
From Animal Stories by Stephen Southwold

Rats are very fond of eggs, especially hens' eggs and will steal them whenever they get the chance.

Quite near my cottage there is a shop kept by Mr Collins. Now Mr Collins is a very jolly man and has many friends who like to bring him presents of eggs. But Mr Collins also has many rats in his shop and they do not always stay in the shop but come into the living room and once even came up to the bedroom. Well, one evening a friend brought round a big paper bag with 12 fine hens' eggs inside. While they sat and talked, Mr Collins put the bag of eggs on the mantelpiece and forgetting it when he went to bed left it there all night. In the morning the bag was there but it was empty. The rats had taken every egg but how they managed to get them down without breaking a single one is a puzzle.

I told this story to a friend of mine and he laughed and said, "I think I can help with the puzzle."

"Well?" I asked.

"Well," he went on, "I was once out walking in a lane near a farmyard and hearing a scuffling in the hedge, went to see what it was all about. There I saw a big rat lying upon his back and clasping an egg in his paws, while another rat pulled him along by his tail."

I laughed. "I don't think that helps very much," I said, "for how did they get down from the mantelpiece?"

My friend shook his head and then said, "I once saw rats carry over 40 eggs down a long flight of stairs. I was staying in an old farmhouse and many 100s of eggs were stored in the loft to be packed the next day and sent out. My bedroom was next to the loft and during the night I heard much squeaking and scampering.

"I opened my bedroom door and peeped out. It was a moonlit night and I could see everything. On each stair sat a rat. Other rats were taking eggs from the big basket and rolling them over the floor towards the staircase. As soon as an egg reached the top stair the rat sitting there took it in his forepaws and handed it down to the rat below him. And so it went on until the egg was at the bottom of the stairs, when a big rat pushed it towards one of the rat-holes.

"I at once shouted and clapped my hands and the rats scampered in all directions. I then went and woke up the farmer and when he came and counted the eggs left he said, "It's a good job you heard them for the little wretches have already taken 40 and by the morning would have had the lot."

COCKERELS

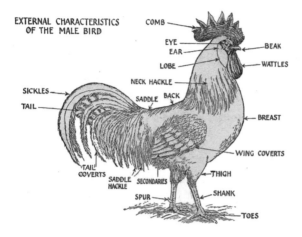

EXTERNAL CHARACTERISTICS
OF THE MALE BIRD

You do not need to have a cockerel if you are a beginner and you will probably be advised to start with four hens. However later on you may acquire a cockerel and you will need one if you want to hatch chicks on a regular basis. Otherwise you may be able to buy fertile eggs to put under a broody hen. You may decide a cock will be unpopular with your neighbours. We had a cockerel who took to crowing at all hours, even at 2a.m. in the pitch black!

Cockerels do however have some advantages. They can prove surprisingly thoughtful when looking after the hens on their patch, often calling them over to enjoy tasty morsels. I recently watched our Welsummer cockerel spend ages securing one ripe blueberry by poking his beak through some netting – he gently placed it on the ground and called his girls over to enjoy his find.

Cockerels usually do most of their mating between April and October. A cockerel will approach a hen and stand erect in front of her with his neck feathers ruffled. He will then dance around her with the wing nearest her spread downwards. The hen, if a submissive one, will duck down and allow him to mount her. He will use his wings to maintain his balance and grip her by the nape of her neck while he mates (your poor hens may lose some feathers on top of their heads as a result). The cockerel may also be quite cunning, luring his hens over by calling them to food and then jumping on them! The problems with mating occur with the high-ranking hens who will often object to mating by flying off and refusing to let the cock near them. We had one bantam hen called Georgie who was horribly persecuted by a cock. He was always chasing her and she would fly up on to a pergola attached to our house to avoid him – needless to say we had to get rid of him to give her some peace.

You can now buy poultry saddles – you attach these by using straps under your hen's wings and these will protect your hens from being damaged by over-zealous cockerels. It is the claws and spurs of the cockerel which pull out the feathers on the hens' backs, making them sore. These saddles can also be used on hens that are being bullied by other hens, who are at the bottom of the pecking order.

Your main problem when rearing chicks is going to be getting rid of the cockerels. You only really need one cock to 25 hens and since you get an average of 60% male chicks when you hatch a brood, you are almost certain to have to dispose of some of your cockerels. If you are very lucky you may be able to give them away. If you have a pure bred cockerel you may find a breeder who needs one. Otherwise they must be killed. But do make sure there are no small children around when this is done. The old fashioned way is to wring their necks but this is no job for an amateur. To wring the neck you must grip it firmly while you hold the bird by its feet. Pull down on the neck, and then quickly bend it upwards until you feel the neck snap. Make the movement in one strong, fluid motion. After you snap the chicken's neck, the wings will start to flap as a last reflex. In the old days people would then drop the chicken and let it run around before dying. Hence the term: 'run around like headless chickens'. A trip to an obliging vet may be preferable.

AN AESOP FABLE - THE VICTOR VANQUISHED

A cock, which had got the worst of a fight with its rival for the favours of the hens, went and hid in a dark corner, while the victor climbed onto a high wall and crowed at the top of his voice. Immediately an eagle swooped down and snatched him up. The other was safe in his dark hiding place and was now able to woo the hens without fear of interruption.

The moral – God resists the proud but gives grace to the humble.

BROODY HENS AND HATCHING CHICKS

Broody Hens

Firstly, if you have one of the non-sitting breeds such as Welsummer, Ancona, Leghorn or Hamburgh, your hens shouldn't go broody at all. If you have hybrids they tend not to go broody – they have had this particular trait bred out of them, although some hybrids, in particular Black Rocks do sometimes go broody, especially after a couple of years of continuous egg laying. Other hens will generally go broody after they have laid between 12 and 20 eggs if you leave these eggs in their nests. Each hen warms her eggs every time she sits to lay an egg and sits longer as the time for broodiness approaches. Obviously, if you collect the eggs every day, she will not go broody as easily. But hens that go persistently broody are the little Pekins, Silkies and the heavier breeds such as Orpingtons and Brahmas. My Wyandottes also tend to go broody quite frequently. Your hens may become broody two or three times in the spring and summer or even autumn.

Classic symptoms of a broody hen are: firmly sitting on the nest box, reluctant to move, fluffing up her feathers, clucking and pecking you when you try and lift her off, as she doesn't like you interferring with her or her eggs. When out of the nest box she will walk around with fluffed up feathers, clucking and behaving in a bad tempered way. She will eat and drink and then try to get back to her nest box. If you shut her out she will sit outside on the bare ground, often enduring pecks from other hens. To stop your hen being broody, put her in an airy coop with a slatted or wire mesh floor where there is no opportunity for nesting. Ideally after a few days isolated in a coop, she will give up feeling broody and, if you then feed her on layers pellets, she should start laying again quite quickly.

If you are allowing your hen to go broody on eggs she has laid in her own nest, she will automatically make her own storage conditions. Brooding is quite a secretive process for a hen and she will have chosen the darkest corner that she can find. If she is allowed to free range this could mean she has made a nest hidden away in the undergrowth in a corner of your garden, where she may have laid a substantial number of eggs – I once had a hen whom I eventually found trying to sit on 36 eggs in a neighbour's garage! If you have a cockerel and so plenty of fertile eggs and one of your hens has gone broody but you have collected her eggs in the days beforehand then you need to put all the fertile eggs you want her to hatch under her at the same time.

If your hen has gone broody in an unsuitable spot (she could be vulnerable to predators) you will need to move her and her eggs to a safe nesting box. This can be tricky; she may not be happy and may return to the old nest - try and do it at dusk and she may settle; watch her the next day when she comes off her nest to feed and drink - make sure she returns to her new nest.

Sitting on the eggs

If you don't have a cockerel but want to hatch some chicks, you can buy fertile or hatching eggs from poultry keepers or from the Domestic Fowl Trust to put under a broody hen. First make sure she is definitely broody and has been sitting, after you have moved her to a secure nesting spot, either on crock eggs or some of your eggs for two or three days. She won't like you interfering with her or her eggs – she may peck you. If you check her in the evening and she is still sitting, this is a good indication that she is broody. You can use a pullet as a broody but you should make sure that she has been laying for at least two months before you allow her to sit. You should delouse your broody hen with louse powder at this point as you don't want her disturbed by fleas as she sits. No one can of course guarantee the fertility of the eggs so use more eggs than the number of chicks that you want, so as not to be disappointed. You should put an odd number of eggs underneath her as these make a circle. About nine eggs is enough for a small bantam, but a larger hen can sit on up to 15 eggs. It is important to allow any fertile eggs that you have ordered to rest for 12 hours after transportation. Eggs can be stored for up to 10 days before starting incubation. If you are using your own eggs, make sure they are an average size and good shape. If you are storing fertile eggs until you have enough to set under the hen together, they should not be too hot, as embryonic development will start at 20°C (68°F) or above, or too cold. An optimum temperature is around 13°C (55°F). You should store them pointed end down or on their side and you should turn them once a day; this is to stop the embryo from floating upwards and adhering to the shell membrane. Do not wash the eggs unless they are dirty, in which case you should use warm water. Place the eggs under your broody hen in the evening when she is calm.

Once a day your hen will need to leave her nest to eat, drink, defecate and take a dust bath. She should not be off the eggs for more than about 20 minutes but don't worry if it is longer. The eggs will cool off during this time but this is important for their development as it allows fresh air into the eggs. If she is reluctant to leave her nest each day you should gently pick her up, taking care that no eggs are concealed between her wings or feathers, and take her to where you have placed food and water. It is a good idea to check the eggs when your broody hen comes off the nest and if any have broken you must remove them. Also you should wash any eggs that have become stained in warm water before returning them to a clean nest of straw. Check that her feet are clean when she goes back on her nest.

Each day a broody hen will move or turn her eggs – this can happen up to 50 times a day and stops the yolk sticking to the side of the shell as it develops. A small amount of grease from her body is transferred on to the eggs and this helps prevent the loss of moisture during storage.

You should feed your hen a diet of mixed poultry corn while she is sitting. Layers' pellets are unsuitable as they pass through her digestive system too quickly and cause her to defecate on the eggs. The maize in the mixed grain is particularly important as it is full of protein.

Hatching chicks

Bantam eggs usually hatch before those of a hen, taking between 18 to 20 days rather that the 21 days for a hen. The chick will start cheeping while still inside its egg and this will trigger the hen's maternal instincts. Shortly before hatching, the chicks take in the yolk sac via the umbilical cord which then closes up. The chick will then raise its head and the egg-tooth on top of the beak will press a hole in the shell, causing the egg to crack open and the chick to hatch.

If you have bought day-old-chicks which you want your broody to foster, you need to introduce them during the first night after *her* eggs have hatched, otherwise she will not accept them. Her maternal instinct is very strong and the first day is rather like a photograph – she has good colour vision and will accept various different coloured chicks but only on that first day. She cannot count but that photograph of her chicks will be imprinted on her brain and if you try and add a new chick on the third day she will not accept it and may even kill it. Silkies are the exception - they will accept chicks at any time. You can use a pullet as a broody but you should make sure that she has been laying for at least two months before you allow her to sit. It is not a good idea to mix bantam and large fowl chicks due to the difference in size and the obvious risk of bullying.

If eggs under your broody still remain unhatched after 21 days you can test them by placing them in a bowl of hand hot water. Those that sink then bob about after a few seconds contain live chicks and should be put back under your hen. If after a couple of minutes there is no sign of life they should be discarded. You can also shake the eggs and if you can detect liquid inside you will know these have not developed either.

If your hen has started to sit on eggs and some have been added later, because for example another hen has laid on her nest while she has been taking her 20 minute break, this can be a problem. Once her chicks have hatched and are up and about, Mother Hen may not be able to keep the remaining eggs warm. However I heard a lovely story the other day – a clever little cross breed had rolled the unhatched eggs around with her as she sat with her chicks in a different area of her run and lo and behold after a couple of days she hatched these too!

There is a lot of information here about what you should and shouldn't do for your broody hen and her nest. If your hens are totally free range, they may not need any help in producing a brood of chicks. My little black Wyandotte cross disappeared a couple of years ago and I found her two days before her 13 chicks hatched.

Feeding and Rearing the Chicks

Chicks do not need anything to eat for at least the first 24 hours because the yolk in their stomachs gives them all the nourishment they need during this period. While her chicks are hatching, Mother Hen will sit for approximately 48 hours and manage without food or water. You should try and leave her alone for this period.

Then start your chicks on chick crumbs, which they need to eat for the first six to eight weeks. You can also give them breadcrumbs mixed with chopped up boiled eggs. Mother

Hen will be happy to eat the chick feed as she gradually regains her strength after days of semi-starvation. Newly born chicks should be fed every couple of hours. Drinking water is also very important.

In the past people used a specially designed rearing coop in which the hen stays behind bars and cannot disturb the chicks as they feed, drink and run about. I find this method unnecessary and rather unnatural. It is true that your hen might become quite agitated once she is up and about, scratching the feed all over the place, upsetting the water and scattering her chicks in the process. It is therefore best not to put hay or straw in the coop once the chicks have hatched, as Mother Hen will scratch that up too and may inadvertently kick her chicks and kill or injure them. A simple, small hen house with run attached will be ideal to accommodate hen and chicks. In any case, if you are moving your brood to new quarters, leave this until the evening about 24 hours after they have all hatched.

Mother Hen will teach her chicks all they need to know about life and I usually let her out for a good dust bath around two weeks after the chicks have hatched. The chicks will quickly learn how to dust bathe themselves at this time as well.

After about five weeks the chicks will have grown enough feathers not to need to sleep under Mother Hen any more, although they may still want to. At around eight weeks the broody hen will slowly lose her attachment to her chicks and return to the flock. She may at this time turn suddenly against the male chicks in particular, and start pecking them. Her maternal instincts disappear and her hormones are now geared for egg laying and she may start laying eggs almost straightaway. The brood of chicks however will tend to stick together once their Mum leaves.

Meanwhile, your chicks will not become sexually mature until 21 weeks. They then may start laying eggs but everything depends on the time of the year that they hatched. If the days are shortening when they reach sexual maturity then they may not start laying until the following spring. If they have been born in February for example then they may start laying in July.

MOST POPULAR BREEDS
Including some of the most important breeds for creating Hybrids

ARAUCANA

Araucanas were bred by the Indians from the Arauca Province of Northern Chile, South America, who refused to let the Spanish conquerors crossbreed their hens. They are the only hens in the world to lay turquoise eggs (colours vary between green, olive and blue) but no one knows quite why they do. Araucanas are crested and have faces covered with thick muffling. They have pea combs with an often irregular slightly twisted shape and come in many colours including lavender, blue, silver, black and white. There is also a Rumpless variation of the breed which, as the name suggests, does not have a tail but is favoured because it lays a large egg in relation to its body size. In fact in America the standard Araucanas are Rumpless. The breed has only become popular relatively recently. The Araucana can be successfully crossed with other breeds and the eggs will still be blue or green, due to a dominant gene – crossing with white egg layers tends to result in blue eggs, while crossing with brown egg layers tends to result in khaki green eggs. Araucanas are quite flighty and like to roam and so may not be ideal for small gardens. They are available as large fowl or bantams and are a light soft-feathered breed. The autosexing breed, Cream Legbars, have been developed using Araucanas crossed with Leghorns. (These are bred so that female and male chicks can be distinguished by colour).

BRAHMA

The Brahma is a very old breed supposedly from India and early pictures show that it was very similar to the Cochin from China. The name Brahma is taken from the river Brahmaputra in India. However, it is now generally agreed that the Brahma was created in America from Shanghais or Cochins imported from China in the 1800s and crossed with Grey Chittagongs (Malay type birds from India). It is known that a crate of nine Brahmas was sent to Queen Victoria in 1852 from the American breeder Burnham and thus the breed was introduced to Britain. Brahmas have distinctive feathered legs and feet and a pea comb. They come in a variety of types and colours including dark, buff, light, birchen and dark Columbian. They are a heavy, soft-feathered breed and lay tinted eggs. Brahmas are very large – they have a sort of majestic massiveness and have been variously described as 'noble and commanding', 'intelligent looking', 'with a neck well proportioned and finely curved as in a spirited horse'. Buff Brahmas are probably the most popular variety. Brahmas can weigh from 5kg (11lb) to 6kg (13lb) so are not ideal for small children. They do need space but, because they don't fly, are easy to keep in a run. They have been used in the creation of many new breeds and in developing new colours in existing ones.

COCHIN AND PEKIN

The Cochin originally came from China in the 1850s where it was known as the Shanghai. It originally had clean legs and became very popular in this country owing to its size and laying powers. However exhibition breeders turned the Cochin into a 'bag of feathers' and it eventually lost its good name. Now similar to the Brahma with feathered legs and feet, it is a heavy soft-feathered breed and lays tinted eggs. There are no miniatures of this bird but Pekin bantams are a similar small version.

The Pekin was introduced to Britain from China. In 1860 the summer palace of the Chinese Emperor at Pekin was sacked by English and French forces and some Pekin Bantams were brought home to England as plunder. The Pekin was originally thought to be a miniature of the Cochin, but in reality has no connection with it. Pekins are a genuine bantam breed and are small with feathered feet and are a wonderful tame breed for children. They are popular as they look round and cuddly. They come in a variety of colours including black, blue, buff, white, cuckoo, lavender and partridge. They don't lay particularly well and the eggs are small, being light beige. The hens go broody frequently which is fine if you want to hatch some eggs but annoying if you don't, since they are very persistent about remaining broody. Their disadvantage is that the feathered feet tend to get wet and muddy very easily. However the advantage is they won't scratch up your garden as they are hindered by their feathered feet. They will need dry conditions for perching so that their leg feathers can dry. The advantage of keeping Pekin cockerels is they crow quite softly.

LEGHORN

A very popular light breed which originated from the Port of Leghorn in Italy and was imported into Britain in the late 1800s, with white first and then brown Leghorns. Leghorns have had the longest life of any of the productive breeds ever introduced. It was a light bird originally and there is evidence from old pictures that this type of bird with a flop-over comb in the female was to be found in many countries of Europe. Old breeds such as the Belgian Brakel, Pheasant Fowls and the Scots Grey had similar features such as white earlobes, flop-over combs and laid white eggs. It is possible therefore that this Mediterranean type was the original fowl of Europe and that the heavier type of Leghorn evident today was due to crossing Malays, Cochins and Minorcas. Prolific layers of white eggs, Leghorns are a light, soft-feathered breed and non-sitters. There are now other colour variations available such as black, barred, buff, cuckoo, mottled and partridge, and bantams are miniatures of their large fowl counterparts. Leghorns are used extensively to produce a variety of hybrids.

MARANS

English ships sailing into Marans in France, near La Rochelle, in the 1800s used to carry hens and fighting cocks. These were exchanged with fresh hens from Marans and the region became the birthplace of a particular breed of poultry, originally called the Marandaise, later to become the Marans. Around 1880 two brothers, poultry merchants from London, were responsible for spreading knowledge of the Marans hens. One of them was a wholesaler of white Russian eggs (Russia was at this time an important poultry producing country). The other brother, whose ships docked at Marans, had the idea of competing with the white Russian egg trade by selling the dark brown eggs of Marans hens which were bigger and fresher. Thus the eggs soon became popular in the London markets. Maranses were crossed with Brahmas and Langshans in order to make the eggs browner – Brahmas were used for their egg laying abilities and the Langshans for the dark brown colour of their eggs.

Maranses weren't actually introduced to Britain until 1929. They are a heavy breed and are the one breed where it is relatively easy to distinguish male and female chicks – males have a white spot on the top of their heads while females have a darker one. They lay very large deep brown eggs and are a good choice of breed for free range as they forage well. Bantams are available as miniatures of their large fowl counterpart. The cuckoo coloured variety is the most popular. They can look similar to the Barred Plymouth Rocks. Maranses' eggs are so special that in France competitions are held on the size, shape, texture and dark colour . The colour ranges from brown to a dark chocolate. Bantams are usually not that tame and not particularly keen on being touched. Hens are large and heavy. I have heard that they can be unreliable layers but worth keeping just for the colour of the eggs.

ORPINGTON

Orpington fowl were named after a village in Kent where William Cook first bred them in the late 1800s. Langshans, Minorcas and Plymouth Rocks were involved in its creation and today they still look similar to the Langshan. The black variety was followed by the white and then the buff. There is now a blue variety as well. Orpingtons are compact with short legs and classified as a heavy soft-feathered breed. Bantams are also available in this breed and are very popular as they are docile and good with children. The Queen Mother used to keep large fowl Buff Orpingtons. The Black Orpington was re-introduced to this country from Australia in the 20s and called the Australorp. A later introduction was the Jubilee Orpington, which is rarely seen but has recently been added to the breeds at the Domestic Fowl Trust. Orpingtons are large, heavy and rather broad with an abundance of feathers which makes them look even bigger. They do not fly because of their weight so are easily kept within the garden. They lay well and their eggs are light brown – however the eggs are smaller than you would expect when you look at the size of the hens.

RHODE ISLAND RED

The Rhode Island Red originated in America on the farms of the Rhode Island Province and they were developed from Red Malays crossed with brown Leghorns. They were first exhibited in 1880 in South Massachusetts and in 1909 the British Rhode Island Red Club was established. The breed has been one of the most popular in this country for all purposes especially in the past when people kept hens for meat as well as for eggs. The male, being a gold, is particularly useful for crossing with hens and is used extensively nowadays for the development of the many hybrids on the market. Eggs are light brown or brown in colour.

Rhode Island Reds along with Sussexes and Leghorns were the breeds that people kept on a more commercial basis during and between the wars. Rhode Island Reds are used in many of the hybrids now on the market.

SUSSEX

This is an old breed derived from the Old Sussex fowls which were bred in Victorian times for their meat and eggs. The oldest variety is in fact the Speckled Sussex. The Light Sussex was developed using Brahmas, Cochins and Dorkings. The Sussex is a heavy soft-feathered breed which lays tinted eggs. During the war Light Sussexes along with Rhode Island Reds seem to have been popular breeds to keep for the dual purpose of eggs and meat. Nowadays Buff and Silver Sussexes are popular colours and are available as bantams or as large fowl. Nowadays the Sussex is also used to produce a sex linked hybrid.

SILKIE

Silkies originated in Asia, some believe in India, others think in China or Japan. They are famous for their broodiness and are covered in fine, silky fluff rather than feathers. Silkies are crested with feathers on the legs and they have five toes. Colours range from blue, gold and black to white and partridge. Ear lobes should rightly be turquoise and comb and wattles mulberry. Silkies are classified as a light soft-feathered large fowl but a small bantam version has been created which is docile and therefore popular with children.

Silkies are well known for making fantastic surrogate mothers. Unlike other breeds they will take on other chicks, even ducklings and don't mind when you add them to their brood. In times gone by, before incubators existed, Silkies were used as natural incubators by breeders not only of chickens, but also of pheasant, partridge and duck.

WELSUMMER

Although Welsummers are traditionally associated with Welsum in Holland the breed was originally created in the area along the river Ysel, just north of Deventer. The breed was developed in the early 1900s, about the same time as the Barnevelders. In the early development of the breed Barnevelders were used. Welsummers arrived in England around 1928. A light, soft-feathered breed, they lay large dark brown eggs with a matt shell rather than the glossy shell of the Marans. The colour of the eggs will vary slightly depending on the strain but these are probably the darkest brown of all egg layers. Welsummer can prove a good choice since they lay well and do not usually go broody. If you want a good looking cockerel you can't do much better than a Welsummer cockerel – they are the traditional Kelloggs Cornflakes cockerels with beautiful plumage. The silver duckwing cockerel is also outstandingly handsome and features on the cover of this book.

WYANDOTTE

The first variety of the Wyandotte was the silver-laced and it originated in America named after a tribe of North American Indians. The Wyandotte tribe still have a few members living in Northern Oklahoma today. It is not absolutely clear which breeds were used to develop the Wyandotte but it was probably Cochins. The Wyandotte was introduced into Britain in the late 1800s and in the early 1900s was very popular along with the Leghorn as an egg laying breed.

There are a variety of colours available nowadays which include gold, buff and blue-laced, partridge, Columbian and silver-pencilled. Varieties have been developed by crossing different breeds with Wyandottes – for example the partridge Cochin and gold-spangled Hamburgh males were crossed with silver-laced females to produce the gold-laced varieties and the Columbians came about by crossing white Wyandottes with Brahmas. In recent times the Wyandotte bantams have become more popular than the large fowl. They are so pretty that I think they make an excellent choice for the garden.

Wyandottes are a heavy, soft-feathered breed and lay tinted eggs. They tend to have lots of fluffy down feathers round their behinds which add to their attractiveness. They go broody rather easily and can be very persistent about it. However they make excellent mothers. Wyandotte bantams are a good choice if you have children as they tend to be friendly and easily tamed. The cocks are not aggressive and in general the bantams are not flighty and easily confined if you have no alternative.

HYBRIDS

There are many hybrids now on the market which have been bred to be specifically good at egg laying but after two years of intensive laying, production of eggs will decrease. Hybrids were originally developed for intensive production and kept in battery conditions – the brown egg layers were based on the Rhode Island Red and the white egg layers on the White Leghorn. These have various trade names such as Shaver and ISA. Isa Warrens and Isa Browns are brown-feathered hybrids that have been specifically bred for free range.

Recently other hybrids have also been developed for free range conditions and also to look attractive in the garden. One of the most successful is the Black Rock. They are a true first cross hybrid, bred from selected strains of Rhode Island Reds and barred Plymouth Rocks. Peter Siddons of Muirfield Hatchery in Scotland acquired the breeding stock from breeders in America in 1973. He remains the sole breeder. The gold feathered genetics of the Rhode Island Red are crossed with the silver feathered lines of the Plymouth Rock and you get a sex linkage feature that identifies each sex when the chicks hatch. This is why there are no Black Rock cockerels. The female chicks are sent out to the agents who bring them on and sell them at POL (Point of Lay). Black Rocks have a good covering of feathers which protect them in all weather conditions. They also have a highly developed immune system and seem to be less prone to red mite than other breeds. They love being outside in all weathers.

Black Rocks do not go broody as this trait has been bred out of them and although egg production which is fantastic in the first two years may decrease thereafter, Black Rocks are hybrids that do manage to go on producing eggs and may live for up to ten years. They also produce good strong egg shells and this reduces the chances of egg peritonitis which so often occurs in battery hens and some other commercial hybrids. Black Rocks are either black or ginger (with a ginger breast and attractive ginger and black lacing).

There are many other hybrids on the market. Calder Rangers (also known as Columbian Blacktails and used by Waitrose for their free range eggs) are consistently good layers as are White Stars (developed from Leghorns and layers of white eggs). Bovans Nera, Hebden Black and the Speckledy are all hybrids worth considering. Meadowsweet Poultry Services have agents across the country and their range includes Black Star (Rhode Island Red crossed with barred Plymouth Rock), Bluebelle (a Marans and Rhode Island Red cross and a layer of dark brown eggs) and Speckled Star (French Cuckoo Marans, also a layer of dark brown eggs) and White Star (a Leghorn Hybrid). All these hens lay between 220 and 320 eggs a year. There is another group of poultry suppliers selling a relatively newly named group of hybrids – they have names such as Fenning Black and Fenning White, Medlesham Blue (similar to Bluebelle), Fenning Coucou (French Marans hybrid), Suffolk Blacktail (a Rhode Island Red hybrid) and Suffolk Noir (a black Copper Marans hybrid). Eden Livestock sell their range of hybrids (based again on Rhode Island Red, Sussex, Marans and Leghorn) and they are named Coral Nova, Amber Nova, Blue Nova (similar to Bluebelle), Cuckoo Nova (from Cuckoo Marans), Sussex Nova and Silver Nova and Columbine (blue egg layer).

There are also various autosexing breeds that have been developed and their names all end in –bar. These have been bred so that chicks can be sexed as soon as they have hatched by their down colouring. The first of these was the Cambar and was a cross between the Gold Campine and the barred Plymouth Rock. The barring is sex-linked and there is a double dose in the male and a single dose in the female – this means the male chick is paler with a blurred pattern of markings compared to the female chick. Recognised breeds are the gold, silver and cream Legbar (the Cream Legbar is a crossing which involves the Araucana and therefore lay blue eggs); the Rhodebar (from Rhode Island Red); Welbar (from

Welsummer) and Dorbar (from Dorking - an old breed which traditionally has five toes). The Crested Cream Legbars have been used to breed a blue egg laying hybrid called Columbine or Skyline. These birds are typically reddish brown partridge feathered, some with crest and some without. They usually have quite a large comb but you are warned that the probability of blue egg colour from these hybrids is usually 85%.

Your hybrids could live up to 10 years and might continue to lay some eggs every year after the two year pretty intensive egg laying period. I have a six year old Black Rock who lays very well through the spring and summer; however the other Black Rock that I acquired at the same time does not lay at all. So it's a bit of a lottery as to how long your hens will lay and how long they will live. Hybrids can suffer from malformed ovaries and tubes due to intensive breeding and I think this is why the Amber Star I bought a couple of years ago has never managed to lay a proper egg with a shell – she laid shell-less eggs for a time and has now stopped laying completely. You can read more about shell-less eggs on pages 29 and 70.

COMMON PROBLEMS, MITES AND DISEASES

Firstly it must be said that one of your hens may become unwell, refusing to eat and drink and look hunched up, miserable and appear to have no energy. This has happened to several of our hens over the years. A visit to the vet does not always help since diagnosis is quite difficult, if nothing is obviously wrong and we have been told a post-mortem is the only way to find the cause of illness. Most of our hens who have become ill have subsequently died.

Crop Bound - Also called Impacted Crop

Hens only have a small gizzard or stomach for grinding up their food – this is quite a long process as they have no teeth to chew anything up. The food is stored in the crop which will be quite large by the end of the day. During the night the food will gradually go down into the gizzard and the crop will be pretty much empty by the morning. If your hen has an impacted crop it will feel hard and even hang down heavily. If you pick the hen up you will feel a hard ball of food which has accumulated within – often this is a twisted ball of grass which is then too large to pass down. I have heard recommended giving the hen live white maggots to eat – these then dislodge the blockage. Otherwise you can try pouring a lubricant such as a little olive oil down her throat – this is easiest done with a syringe - and if you gently massage the crop, the food should soften and pass through. You can also use liquid paraffin as an alternative to olive oil (olive oil can be bad for the chicken's liver) – apparently liquid paraffin does not go through the liver but passes out with the droppings. Alternatively you could give the hen a drink of warm water, then turn her upside down and gently massage the crop to try and release the blockage. Do not try and make your hen sick as the hard lump will be too big to come back up. Try to feed your hen soft food as you wait for the blockage to clear – you do not want to make it worse. If the impaction does not clear then your best option is to take your hen to the vet – he may make a small incision in her breast and be able to remove the blockage.

Sour Crop

This is another problem that can occur although I have never experienced it. The crop will feel very soft rather like a water filled balloon. Sour crop is caused by a fungal infection and the hen's breath will smell bad. Hold the bird upside down with one hand gripping both legs. Massage the crop, pushing it with your hand from the bottom of the crop up towards the hen's head. Hopefully the liquid will come out through the mouth. Feed with live bio-yoghurt and after a day start the hen on hard feed again.

Scaly Leg Mite

The scaly leg mite lives under the scales of the bird's leg. It is contagious and can be seen in birds of all ages. It may originate from the litter on the floor of your hen house. The scales on the legs become rough, and a chalk-like concretion is formed, which accumulates both between and over the scales. It is

Our Appenzeller hen on the left with a Bluebelle hybrid on the right

Our Araucana bantam hen

Our second Welsummer cockerel

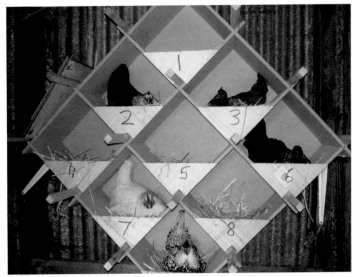

A system of nestboxes hanging in our stable which my husband and son, Tom, made, based on a design we saw at the Barnevelder Poultry Museum in Holland

A little bantam chooses to lay her eggs in a plant pot

Another hen decides to make her nest in a sage bush

A cross breed
bantam with
her little brood
hatched
originally in
secret

Another cross
breed with her
brood

Our buff Pekin with her
brood - chicks love to sit
on their mother's back

Various hens inspecting a raised vegetable box surrounded by a low wire fence

Our silver duckwing Welsummer cockerel amongst the daffodils

Daisy, our
Amber Star
hybrid, posing in
the lavender

Daisy in the compost bin

Dust bathing with chicks

Eating Swiss chard

Enjoying some leftover apple

Relaxing and sunbathing in the sun

Lesiure time - let's see what's going on inside!

intensely irritating to the bird and once developed may make the bird lame and unable to perch. The problem is relatively easy to cure and there are several different treatments you can try. In the past I have used surgical spirit, which you can paint on the legs with a small paintbrush - the surgical spirit will kill many of the mite; if you then cover the legs with vaseline this should suffocate remaining mite and their young. You need to repeat this treatment once a week for four or five weeks to kill off any hatching eggs. Other treatments include scaly cream which is available in pet shops (used for budgies with scaly face); eucalyptus oil which is an organic treatment and must be rubbed into the legs every few weeks; paraffin (an old fashioned remedy) with which you can scrub the legs using an old toothbrush (one treatment should be enough); dipping the legs in linseed oil, which reduces the irritation, softens the scales and promotes healing but you need to repeat this treatment; and lastly for severe cases of scaly leg use Protocon (sulphur based ointment) with which you must cover the legs, then wrap in paper tissue and use tape to keep it in place, leave for at least a week and then you should find the scabs will drop off.

Red Mite

Red mites live and breed in crevices in hen houses. They are carried by wild birds. At night they run along the perches and up the chicken's leg where they suck blood from the flesh. They don't live on the bird but can be spotted during the day – they will be red if they have recently sucked blood, otherwise they will be grey. The chickens affected will look jaundiced through losing blood and will stop laying. Start by ensuring there are as few nooks and crannies as possible. Clean out the hen house. Creosoting is one of the most effective ways of banishing red mite. It has been banned to the general public but is available from agricultural supplies merchants for industrial or professional use which includes for 'agricultural purposes'. If you do use this creosote be sure to let the house air for at least three days afterwards Some people think the new type of creosote such as Cuprinol also works. There are sprays available to kill them such as Poultry Shield. Also quite effective is spraying the hen house with a disinfectant such as Dettol or Jeyes Fluid, limewashing or painting the inside with paraffin. I have also heard of people using cat flea spray or using ant powder such as Nippon on bad patches of red mite. Other products include Invermectin, Frontline and Panacur but they are not licensed for use on poultry unless prescribed by your vet. Another excellent product is Diatom (diatomaceous earth) which can be dusted on everything including your hens and many people swear by it - it has a mechanical action which desiccates the mite. Be aware though that you might have to treat your hen house several times – red mite are notoriously difficult to eradicate completely. They can often get transferred between hen houses either on your body or on a brush or utensil that you have used.

Lice (fleas)

These are irritating for the bird and can be treated by dousing the birds with louse powder. You can also dust the nest boxes and dust baths. Broody hens should also be dusted with powder before sitting.

Worms

There are six different types of worms which can live in the internal parts of chickens. Your hens infected with worms will be listless and have green diarrhoea. You should treat for worms with Flubenvet (available from feed suppliers) mixed into the feed. However some authorities say that you should treat for worms twice a year whether your hens show symptoms or not and some say that de-worming a healthy hen weakens the system and upsets the natural balance of helpful organisms. I have never wormed my hens and because they have a large area on which to free range they don't seem to be affected.

An excellent website to consult if you want to find out more about poultry diseases is: www.organicvet.co.uk

PREDATORS

Foxes are the most common and dangerous killers of hens and usually strike first thing in the morning or at dusk, although in urban areas foxes seem to be seen more and more wandering around during the day. One often hears stories of foxes killing all the hens a family owns in one go. People wonder why a fox has to kill every hen in sight and only carry off one or two. He only does this because he has been disturbed: left to his own devices he would come back and carry off each carcass to bury as food for the future. I recently heard of a fox who leapt through a window into a stable, killed 20 hens and carried off 15 during the night. He is an opportunist and cleverer than we suppose.

How to solve the fox problem? Many people use electric fencing which seems to prove effective – once the fox has experienced an electric shock he is unlikely to come back. However if you have small children this may not be an option. I recently read about someone who had heard that lion dung was a deterrent but when she rang the zoo to see if she could acquire some, she was told there were rules against distributing it because of possible harmful bacteria. What does seem to work as a very useful deterrent is human urine – so give it a go – sprinkle it in the appropriate areas and it should keep the fox away.

Badgers also kill hens and ducks (as I have experienced several times) but do so strictly at night. They can be particularly vicious, have strong claws and can push their way into insecure hen hutches quite easily. They will also eat any eggs they find, leaving egg shells behind. Badgers will burrow under fences and will often defecate while on your land - easily recognisable - their poo is similar to that of a dog but you will see grains and berries in it. Unfortunately it is illegal to kill badgers – you just have to make sure your hen hutches are sturdy enough to withstand an attack. Mink are rarer but have been known to kill chickens. Rats can easily kill a brood of chicks, as can crows, magpies, stoats or weasels. Sparrow hawks are also dangerous – they have taken our chicks in the past. They can swoop down with frightening speed and carry off a chick, even a teenage chick.

Dogs have attacked and killed my bantams in the past and we had a cat who would steal chicks (plastic bottles half filled with water can apparently deter cats - reflections of themselves on the bottles scares them away). If a dog kills any of your hens you can claim damages against the dog's owner under the Animals Act 1971 – *An Act to make provision with respect to civil liability for damage done by animals and with respect to the protection of livestock from dogs ....*

FREQUENTLY ASKED QUESTIONS

Do I need a cockerel for my hen to lay eggs?
No - you only need a cockerel if you want your hen to sit on her eggs and produce chicks.

What are the best breeds for laying eggs?
Many of the hybrids will lay a good quantity of eggs for at least two years.

When will my hens start to lay eggs?
At Point of Lay between 18 and 22 weeks your hens should start laying. Hybrids will start laying at POL even if you get them in the autumn. However pure breeds will not start laying if they reach POL as autumn is approaching – as the days get shorter pure breeds and cross breeds do not lay.

How many eggs will my hens lay and for how long?
Hybrids will lay almost every day for two years but thereafter the eggs will substantially reduce. Pure and cross breeds will lay for longer but only in the spring and summer.

How do I stop my hen being broody?
Hybrid hens shouldn't go broody as this trait should have been bred out of them. However I hear plenty of stories about Black Rocks and other hybrids such as the Fenning Coucou going broody at regular intervals. If you do have a broody you should take them off the nest and put her in a separate coop with a wire mesh floor to make it as uncomfortable as possible.

CHICKEN RUNS AND VEGETABLE PLOTS

Why is my hen laying soft-shelled eggs?
There could be several reasons for this. If your hen has just started laying she may take time to settle into it. Try making sure she is getting oyster shells as this will help her produce enough calcium for the shell. If the problem persists she could have a defect or a damaged reproduction system.

When and how do I tell if a chick is a young cockerel or a pullet (young hen)?
With some breeds it is easier to tell than with others. The Marans chick is easy. Males have a white blob on their heads. You might have to wait until you witness an attempt at crowing from a young cockerel. Cockerels will generally be taller, with larger combs and start developing tail feathers.

How many hens can a cockerel look after and mate with?
A cockerel can easily cope with 12 hens.

What is the best way to introduce hew hens to an established flock?
Keep them in a separate run for a few days so that they can get used to their new surroundings.

How long will my hens live?
Hens can live for 10 years – cross breeds generally live the longest as they are the hardiest but some hybrids such as Black Rocks are also living until at least 10 years old.

Will I get rats?
You may well get rats but then often households without any hens do as well. Try and make sure you don't leave any food hanging around to attract them and store all your hens' feed in secure dustbins.

PART TWO
GROWING PLANTS ALONGSIDE YOUR HENS

WAYS TO PROTECT YOUR PLANTS

I grow herbs, vegetables, fruit and flowers alongside my hens as season follows season, so the family has year-round vegetables. Vegetable-growing works well with hens. Think back to the Second World War when many families grew their own veg and kept their own chickens successfully. Nothing goes to waste as you can always feed surplus vegetables to the chickens.

First you must plan where you are going to grow your vegetables and how you will protect seedlings and young plants from your hens. You will need to protect some of your vegetables if your hens are free ranging.

Netting everything is an option or building a vegetable cage. Low fences are also an idea – you can get rolls of green, sturdy chicken wire which are 60cm, 2 feet high – hens can't really fly over these - hens fly onto fences such as post and rails because they can perch on the rails on their way over but they can't perch on chicken wire! Alternatively you can buy or make raised vegetable boxes, use tunnels, cloches, containers or invest in hanging baskets.

Some people mulch around precious plants with rough gravel or use crinkly lawn edging to protect small plants. Another idea is to use a clipped edging of box or rosemary but this would, obviously, take some time to develop.

71

Tunnels and cloches

There are various types of tunnels on the market, made with polythene or fleece all designed to protect against pests as well as the weather. There are new Ecogreen giant growing tunnels on the market made with aerated polythene, micromesh or a fleece and tinted green to blend in to the environment. They have drawstring ends and are designed to keep off rabbits and pigeons and no doubt will also protect your precious greens from scavenging hens. There are also sturdy cloches available made with clear plastic or you can make your own and cover with polythene.

Raised Vegetable Boxes

You can buy instant raised bed kits – these are usually plastic sided pieces that fit together to make a 1m, 3ft square box which is about 30cm, 1ft high. The kits come with joining pegs that are hammered into the ground. You can then buy support frames separately and put netting over these if you have hens free ranging in your garden. Alternatively we have found that attaching a small 30cm, 2ft green chicken wire fence all the way round (with nails or staples) works well and your chickens shouldn't be able to fly over this. Once the boxes are in place they can then be filled with soil and compost. If you have access to railway sleepers and are good at DIY then these make a good alternative and can be fixed into place with nails or heavy duty staples. Gravel boards can be screwed onto sunken corner posts.

Another more permanent structure can be built using bricks or stones cemented together but this may require concrete footings. Raised boxes have a number of benefits. They allow a wider range of plants to be grown on difficult soils. Drainage will be improved and the soil will actually warm up more rapidly in the spring. They elevate plants to a convenient working level and it is easier to keep your vegetable plants organised. You will also achieve better production per square metre since the beds don't require a lot of space between rows – you don't walk in the bed at all to sow seeds or to harvest your crops. This also means there will be little soil compaction – water, air and roots can all be compressed by human feet treading down soil. Slugs and snails shouldn't find their way into raised beds either which can be a huge bonus.

Hanging Baskets and Containers

These are great for growing tomatoes and some types have been specially developed for hanging baskets. Hens do like ripe tomatoes although will not eat tomato leaves which are poisonous. You can also grow strawberries in hanging baskets to keep them out of reach and even small lettuces such as little gem and other salad leaves. You could also try radishes (hens will eat the radish leaves).

You can grow most vegetables in containers but you will still have to put them in places inaccessible to your hens or have them elevated out of reach. Potatoes can be grown in two or three car tyres piled one on top of another. You can make wooden boxes at least 30cm, 1 ft wide and deep - don't forget the drainage but put holes and some stones in the bottom of your containers.

Grow bags

Grow bags are ideal for trailing plants such as courgettes and squashes and hens won't eat these once the plants are well established. Tomatoes work very well in grow bags – you can also buy grow boxes into which you can put grow bags - they have a wooden frame at the back to support tomato or other plants.

This diagram shows how the system with hens and vegetables in your garden works:

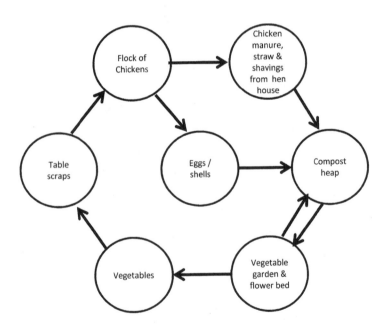

HENS' LIKES AND DISLIKES IN THE GARDEN

PLANTS THAT HENS LOVE AND PLANTS THAT ARE CHICKEN-PROOF

To a large extent what hens will eat in your garden depends on how much access to grassy areas they have. The more land they have to free range, the more likely they are to feast on weeds, wild herbs and grass; it follows therefore that they are less likely to eat your precious plants, flowers and herbs.

I can't stress enough how important grass is – I bought a couple of new hybrids recently; they were already 22 weeks and had been kept inside a barn. When I got them home they were put in a run with grass and they just went mad for it, pecking at the grass ferociously as though it was going to be taken away from them at any moment. If your hens have only a little space to roam around and a small area of grass and greenery they will very soon have eaten all the grass and anything else that is green.

It follows that if you keep your hens enclosed and let them out to free range every so often they will eat anything that's green including vegetables, herbs, weeds, beech hedges and some of your flowers!

Vegetables

Vegetables that your hens probably won't touch include carrots, parsnips, leeks, onions, potatoes, squashes, pumpkins and courgettes. Climbing French and runner beans should be fine once the plants are established as they won't be able to reach most of the beans (you need to protect seedlings as hens will scratch up the earth around them, maybe using a cold frame). They will love eating the sweet corn off the cobs that you don't want. You could also think about growing some sunflowers and feed them the seeds in the autumn.

Hens love spinach, chard, kale, broccoli and cabbage leaves and most forms of lettuce except for the spicy oriental leaves; beetroot leaves are particularly relished and my hens also nibble away at the actual beetroot if I leave one on the ground by mistake. I have also heard of hens who rather like cucumbers although the skin is not meant to be that good for them.

My hens are particularly keen on Jerusalem artichokes which I let them nibble on when I have a huge surplus in the winter months. They shouldn't, however, be tempted to eat the leaves so this is a good vegetable to devote some space to – I've just read about some hens that do eat artichoke leaves – however this doesn't matter as it won't affect the tubers!

Berries and Fruits

Remember that hens are descended from Jungle Fowl who used to survive on green stuff, berries, nuts, grubs etc in the forests. Your hens will be keen on most edible berries. For fruit we grow raspberries which we net for protection against wild birds. Some of my hens manage to pinch the raspberries growing lower down but there are certainly enough to go round. Strawberries are grown under netting and would be eaten if my hens could find a way through. Blackcurrants don't appeal but the bushes provide perfect shelter from the summer sun. Redcurrants do appeal to birds and hens alike so you may have to net these or erect a small fence around the bushes at ripening time. Blueberries are very popular with all birds and so I make sure these are well netted – however the small birds are very determined and usually find their way through a gap and polish off any nearly ripe blueberries. The hens also enjoy the small and bitter grapes from our vine. My hens like autumn fruits such as apples, pears, plums or damsons but obviously these are still safe while on the trees.

Your hens will also enjoy wild blackberries – you can always give them any surplus that you have picked; they will eat rowanberries, rosehips and elderberries although these are thought to be toxic to hens (this is controversial topic - see also page 79). They will eat rhubarb leaves which are said to be toxic to hens as they contain oxalic acid - probably best to protect your rhubarb, although my hens have eaten the leaves in the past to no ill effect.

Flowers, Herbs and Shrubs

For flowers, we tend to do hanging baskets and put pots out of reach of the chickens. The daffodils and tulips don't get touched. Violas, grape hyacinths, myrtle and penstemon are usually safe, too. Shrubs such as spiraea, honeysuckle, magnolia, forsythia, hydrangea, buddleia, rhododendron and mahonia are all unlikely to be eaten by chickens as are ferns, laurel, holly, box, juniper and flowering currant. Other flowers hens shouldn't be interested in include chrysanthemems, irises, kerria, peony, fritillaria, broom, agapanthus and jasmine. I have read on forums people worried about privet and its berries which are poisonous. In my experience chickens wouldn't be tempted to eat these. On the whole they won't touch anything that they don't fancy. They know what to eat and what not to eat.

Hens shouldn't touch the following: sea holly or sea buckthorn, holly, box, ivy, conifer, bay trees, lavender, eucalyptus, lilac, laburnum, laurel, bamboo, carex grass or other tall grasses. Obviously trees such as hazel, hawthorn, elder, rowan, yew, gorse or fruit trees are of no interest to chickens especially as the foliage is generally out of their reach anyway.

A variety of plants are listed as being toxic to hens but they are unlikely to be interested in eating them – these include buttercups, daffodils, tulips, foxgloves, euphorbia (crown of thorns), ivy, hyacinths, oleander, nightshade, rhododendrons and hemlock. Your hens are unlikely to show an interest in flowers such as asters, roses, camellias, dahlias, fuschias, jasmine, azaleas, agapanthus, hydrangeas, viburnums and osmanthus. Hebe is a controversial one – some hens eat it and some don't as with buddleia – some eat it when it's young.

Strong smelling herbs are not an attractive food for hens (see section on herbs on pages 101 - 104)

Plants that Hens Find Particularly Tasty

Some of these I found through lists on forums, listed as irresistible to chickens: chamomile, perennial geraniums, hollyhocks, nasturtiums and in particular the seeds, busy lizzies, lobelia, pansies and hostas – lots of people said these were popular. It was also mentioned that chickens ate delphiniums; however these are also listed as poisonous to chickens on one website that I looked at. I read of someone whose chickens ate lily-of-the-valley which is on the poisonous plants list; so are elderberries although my chickens eat them with no ill effects as do other people's chickens. Tomato leaves are meant to be poisonous but again I have read of chickens eating these. Interestingly we have a beech hedge in the garden which the hens do not touch; however I have noticed a neighbour's hens, which are enclosed with no grass, have stripped all the leaves off the beech hedge bordering their run, as far up as they can reach. Other flowers that chickens will tuck into include marigolds (the petals will make their yolks even yellower); violets, border pinks and sweet peas – I would be surprised if any of these lasted for long in your garden! My borage flowers have not been eaten although I know some hens enjoy these too.

Of course they are always exceptions and reading remarks on the forums I found it extraordinary what some people's chickens were eating - plants that my hens wouldn't even glance at. Some hens eat parsley and lavender which mine have never touched. On the whole hens seem to leave alone strongly scented or aromatic leaves but will eat anything that tastes similar to grass.

OTHER USES HENS HAVE IN THE GARDEN

WEEDS

Hens love chickweed (named because chicks loved it). It is one of the most useful weeds to have in your garden although once you let it develop it grows everywhere – feed it to your chickens or you can also use it yourself in salads. Your hens will eat dandelion leaves, comfrey, sorrel, horseradish leaves and dock leaves if desperate. Chickens unfortunately will not eat nettles (although some hens do eat wilted nettles), bindweed, plantain, moss, ground elder, mallow or anything that is too bitter or too strong such as hairy bittercress. I sometimes see mine eating dandelion or dock leaves but these are not their favourites. The dock leaves do contain oxalic acid which is toxic to hens but they probably wouldn't eat dock leaves in huge quantities; fat hen which is similar to good King Henry may also be eaten but again contains oxalic acid. Some hens will eat cleavers and groundsel.

DEVOURERS OF PESTS

Hens will eat many of the insects regarded as garden pests such as woodlice, slugs, snails, leather jackets (larvae of the crane fly), caterpillars, ants and their eggs, beetles and other grubs. In the autumn and winter when I'm digging the garden, the hens are allowed in to the vegetable cages – they love it, fighting over worms and other tasty insects. They also clear up weed seeds, break up clods with their general scratching, deposit some fertiliser as they go and are great company.

POULTRY MANURE

Chicken poo can of course be a nuisance if your hens free range - it gets on one's shoes, on my boys' clothes when they're playing rugby, on the paths and patio. However it doesn't take too long to clear it up and it is supposed to improve the quality of lawn grass.

Poultry droppings make a great fertiliser – add them to your compost heap as an activator – they are full of nitrogen. Fresh poultry manure is generally regarded as too strong to go straight onto vegetable plots. One plant you can apply it directly to is comfrey. You can also put it round your currant bushes as they love nitrogen. Droppings in a water butt produce excellent liquid feed although can prove very smelly!

One hen produces about 5½ kilos or 12lb of manure a year. Moisture content is about 60% and this is why it needs to be dried. It also contains too much nitrogen so in order to use it as a complete manure you would need to add bone meal and potash. If you had 12 kilos or about 25lb of manure you would need to add 3 kilos or 6lb of bone meal and 150g, 6oz of sulphate of potash. An alternative would be to use the dried poultry manure as a nitrogenous fertiliser and apply along rows of brassicas that need extra nitrogen. Apparently a good way of drying poultry manure is to put sedge peat under the perches and then to gather poultry droppings and peat together and store in a compost bin for three months before using. If you don't want to use peat, it is best to dry the droppings as quickly as possible spreading them out on metal trays in a shed and then pulverizing them possibly with the back of a spade.

FEATHERS

Feathers gathered when your hens moult act as a slow release nitrogen fertiliser if you dig them in around your blackcurrants or you can also compost them.

You could also collect up feathers, especially hackles (neck feathers from both hens and cockerels) and give them to any fishermen you know for their flies. If you have a cockerel, his tail feathers when he moults, would also be useful to a fly fisherman.

EASY VEG TO GROW

CROP ROTATION AND
COMPANION PLANTING

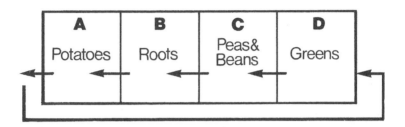

A	B	C	D
Potatoes	Roots	Peas&Beans	Greens

There is a lot written about crop rotation. Here is a summary offering a basic plan. Potatoes are what is called a cleaning crop. The ground needs to be well-manured for potatoes. You should follow potatoes with root crops such as carrots, parsnips and beetroot as these don't need manure. Then the next year you would use the patch for peas and beans. These leave nitrogen in the soil which is excellent for the brassicas and leafy crops which you can plant as soon as you have uprooted the beans. If you were to have four raised beds and you moved the crops each year you would really only have to net or fence the one with the brassicas and greens as your hens wouldn't be interested in the other crops, with the exception of the beetroot. You could grow your onions in the same bed as the potatoes.

There is also much written about companion planting. Many people grow marigolds as they attract hoverflies to prey on the aphids. Nasturtiums are great for attracting greenfly away from your brassicas, peas and beans. If you grow strong smelling herbs amongst your vegetables they will keep various pests away. Grow rosemary near your carrots and the carrot root fly will smell the rosemary rather than the carrots and fly past! Basil will keep flies away from potatoes; chives will deter aphids, mint will keep ants away; garlic will protect potatoes. There are also certain vegetables that like to grow next to other vegetables – onions like to grow with beetroot; carrots grow happily with lettuce and radishes but also do well with onions as the onions (like rosemary) smell strongly and help keep the carrot root fly at bay. All the books say never grow onions with beans and peas – they are incompatible but none of them say why. I finally found some information on a forum – due to the sulphur that onions secrete, the onion family kills off the beneficial bacteria that peas and beans need to have in the soil to fix the nitrogen and grow well. One plant combination that works very well though, is to grow sweet corn, climbing beans and courgettes together. The climbing beans grow up the maize plants, the sweet corn benefits from the nitrogen in the soil that the beans produce and the courgettes grow below with their large leaves which help suppress weeds. Once these plants are established your hens shouldn't bother with them but if you find they are continually scratching up the soil around the plants you could put a circle of low fencing around the patch.

SALAD LEAVES AND ROCKET

There are four types of lettuce: Loose Leaf, Butterhead, Cos and Crisphead. The Loose Leaf are the type that do not form hearts and there are now many varieties of these which are also known as 'cut and come again' - if you pick a few leaves from each plant new ones will form in their place. Butterhead types form a heart but the leaves are soft and delicate. The Cos lettuce forms an upright, elongated heart and takes longer to mature than other types – it is used to make a Caesar salad. The Crisphead, of which the Iceberg and Webb's Wonderful are the best known varieties, takes on the appearance of a cabbage with succulent, crisp and wrinkled leaves. These however tend to be less nutritious with their pale green leaves.

There are so many varieties of lettuce available now that if you plant carefully you can have some type of lettuce growing in your garden all year round. You can start planting seed under cloches in February and you should be eating salad leaves in April/May. You can plant different seeds all through the summer and there are types for autumn sowing such as Winter Density and Rouge d'Hiver which will survive the winter without protection. There are many different coloured lettuces from pale to dark green to green-speckled with red to red-tinted to almost completely crimson. Red Salad Bowl, Lollo Rossa, Amorina and New Red Fire are all red, easy to grow cut-and-come-again lettuces, popular with the children (leaves tend to lose their colour as temperatures rise but become redder in the autumn). There are many oriental leaves on the market – my favourites are golden streaks mustard, red giant mustard, mizuna, mibuna and namenia.

Rocket is very easy to grow, germinating in reasonably low temperatures. The younger leaves are milder and it is best to harvest regularly to prevent the plants bolting. It does run to seed in the summer, preferring cooler temperatures. The flowers are edible and could be added to salads. In seed catalogues it is also known as Roquette or Rucola. Wild rocket is a different species which is more peppery than ordinary rocket but also worth trying.

You will definitely encounter problems with slugs who like eating all salad type leaves and if you don't want to use slug pellets, you can put out beer traps – containers filled with beer which the slugs will be attracted to – you can then feed slugs to your hens. Most of the lettuce that you grow will be enjoyed by your hens – you are bound to have some that's bolted or outside leaves that you don't want to eat – nothing goes to waste when you have hens around!

SPINACH AND CHARD

There are lots of different varieties of spinach and if you choose a couple of summer types and some for autumn planting you will have spinach in late spring and early summer and then again in the winter.

Swiss Chard is a leaf beet and related to beetroot but I have included it with spinach as it is cooked in the same way. Perpetual spinach is also a spinach beet but not a true spinach. There is also another type, New Zealand spinach, which is not a true spinach – it's a spreading, straggly plant but also a tender perennial. True spinach can be divided into two types: summer spinach with round smooth seeds and prickly-seeded varieties which are sown in the autumn and withstand winter conditions. Types to be recommended for the summer are Lazio, Bloomsdale and America. Winter varieties are Giant Winter, Monnopa (this variety has a low oxalic acid content) and Medania - if you sow these in September you will be picking the spinach in April. Perpetual spinach can also be sown in September as it is very winter hardy.

Spinach is easy to grow. The soil should be water retentive, free draining and not too acidic. Soaking spinach seeds overnight before sowing them will speed up germination. They should be sown in rows 30cm, 1ft apart and then thinned to 15cm, 6in apart along the row. Spinach sown in April should be ready for picking in June. Do not allow the plants to dry out - they must be watered regularly. Summer sown spinach can be a problem as it may run to seed before leaves have developed. Spinach definitely prefers cool conditions - you could plant some spinach between rows of peas or beans so that it gets some shade. Of course any damaged outer leaves can be fed to your hens – this is one of their favourite vegetables – spinach does contain oxalic acid but only a small amount so not as toxic as rhubarb!

Chard is a dual purpose vegetable as you can use the stalks separately from the leaves – the stalks can be chopped up and served with butter or a cheesey sauce. Chard is useful since it usually lasts through the winter – it then runs to seed in its second season.

BEANS – BROAD BEANS, MANGE TOUT, SUGAR SNAP PEAS, CLIMBING FRENCH AND RUNNER BEANS

Start the year by planting some broad beans - you can plant the large seeds out in February. These should be put into shallow drills about 6.5cm, 2.5in deep and about 10cm, 4in apart. They like rich soil, preferably manured for a previous crop. Your hens shouldn't be interested in broad bean plants. What you could do is protect young plants with a low fence which you can remove once the plants are well established.

Broad beans make attractive plants in the vegetable garden with their black-spotted white flowers which are particularly attractive to bees that will carry out the job of pollination. Plants can be badly affected by black bean aphids. These flies can stunt growth, damage flowers and ruin the pods. If you pinch off the top 7.5cm, 3in of stem of each plant when the pods first begin to form this may help control the aphids. You can eat these broad bean tops – cook as you would spinach. Broad beans do not need much water except in the case of a drought. The plant is shallow rooted so it is a good idea to earth up around the bases of the plants. They may require some support. Pick pods when the beans begin to show – if picked very young the pods can be eaten whole – leave the pods to become too large and the beans inside will be tough.

Mangetout and sugar snap peas can be sown in late April or early May. Sow 7.5cm, 3in apart. I like to grow these as they are expensive to buy. A good variety to try is Carouby de Maussane which grows like a runner bean plant but has purple flowers and flat thin pods; Oregon Sugar Pods are also popular. Sugar snap peas are fun to grow and can be eaten raw in salads as well as lightly cooked. I particularly like them as they are dual purpose – leave some pods to grow on and then harvest the peas – I love eating these raw – they are so sweet. You should protect the growing plants as birds and mice can devastate a row of germinating peas, and keep them weed free. Do not water in the early stages of growth as this will result in too many leaves - water when the plants begin to flower and when the pods are forming water twice a week to increase the yield. Pick the pods when they are fat but still green and juicy. Both peas and mangetout become available fairly early on in the season, usually June and July. Again you can protect the young plants from your hens with a low fence which you can remove once the plants are growing up either against a higher fence (or you will need to support plants with bamboo canes as they like to attach themselves to something as they grow upwards). Pick the pods regularly when young and the plant will produce more and more young pods.

My climbing French beans usually follow the mangetout and then the runner beans start. I only grow climbing French beans which I find much more productive than the dwarf French beans and again they will be out of reach of foraging hens.

After the broad beans, mangetout and sugar snap peas have finished in August remove all the foliage, leaving the roots in the soil. The nitrogen-producing bacterial nodules on the roots enrich the soil. You can also dig in the broad bean plant stems and leaves. This space is then ready for other crops. It is an ideal spot for brassicas as they benefit especially from the nitrogen that the bean roots release. Alternatively plant winter salads or winter spinach – the nitrogen helps fast growing leafy crops. Since the ground is now full of nitrates it won't need extra fertiliser. You'll be in time to plant some autumn spinach such as Giant Winter when the runner and French beans have finished in September.

ROOT VEG – CARROTS AND PARSNIPS

Carrots do very well in a light sandy soil. Your hens shouldn't be interested in eating the green tops so once established the carrots can be left unprotected. Parsnips will be safe too but you need quite a lot of space for parsnips as they have a long growing season.

Carrots need a light, sandy, free-draining soil. If you are hoping to grow long carrots, the lighter the soil and the fewer stones the better. For the short stumpy varieties most soils will do but it is best not to use fresh manure as this can cause the carrots to fork. Carrots in general do not germinate well if the soil is too cold so it is best to wait until mid spring before sowing seeds. Germination time is usually about 17 days. Carrots sown in May will be ready in September or early October. You will need to thin out the seedlings so that the carrots are about 5 – 7cm, 2 – 3in apart. Carrots should not be over watered as this can lead to rapid leaf growth at the expense of root growth. Nor should carrots be allowed to become too dry especially as, if you then water them extensively, you will cause the roots to split. Varieties to be recommended are Amsterdam Forcing and Early Nantes which are short-rooted early carrots (these can be sown around the end of March). For the maincrop try Chantenay, James Scarlet Intermediate or Autumn King and for late crops try St Valery which is long-rooted or Flakkee which is Dutch and a large thick carrot.

Carrot fly is the most troublesome of pests that can affect carrots. The flies lay their eggs in the soil and the larvae burrow into the carrots. There is no treatment for this problem but there are resistant cultivars on the market. Intercropping carrots with onions can reduce carrot fly. As your carrots develop the sunlight may cause them to go green at the top - if so cover them with a little earth.

The parsnip is a hardy biennial. It needs a deeply cultivated soil which has been manured for a previous crop. As with carrots, parsnips need stone free soil which is moisture retentive in order for the roots to develop fully. They take a long time to germinate (up to 1 month) therefore it is a good idea to sow them interspersed with radishes or with lettuces so that you do not lose track of where you have planted them. Seeds do not keep well so it is best to buy fresh seed every year. Even fresh seeds germinate irregularly so it is best to sow about 5 seeds in a cluster and then thin the seedlings that do develop. Traditionally parsnips are sown in February but in practice it is best to wait until March or April when the soil is warmer and you can even postpone until May and still get a good crop in late November. Seeds should be planted 1cm, $\frac{1}{2}$in deep and depending on the variety of parsnips you use, should be in rows 30cm, 1ft apart for larger roots and 20cm, 8in apart for small types. Thin to 15cm, 6in apart for large varieties and 8cm, 3in apart for smaller varieties. The seeds are very thin like confetti, and consist of a very thin membranous disc which can, in cold soil, become covered with fungus and therefore fail to germinate. Seeds sown in March will produce parsnips ready for harvesting in October/November so they will occupy your patch for a long time. You should not encounter too many problems once the roots start to develop and will only need to hoe and weed between the parsnips. In any case leave your parsnips in the soil until they have been exposed to a couple of frosts as this will improve their flavour. Parsnip canker can develop when wet weather in the autumn follows a particularly dry spell – this causes the crown of the root to crack which may then be invaded by fungi causing the root to go black and rot. Recommended varieties are Avonresister (which is resistant to canker) Tender and True, Gladiator and White Gem.

BEETROOT

Beetroot is easy to grow and although you can use the beetroot leaves in salads, you can also give the larger leaves to your chickens – they love them. You will have to protect these plants – my hens even peck into the raw beetroot if I leave them on the ground after harvesting. There are various types and shapes that you can grow. Of the globe or round shapes, Boltardy is probably one of the best to grow as it is an early cropper and is resistant to bolting. There are also tapered varieties and there is Barbabietola di Chioggia, an Italian type that has unusual white rings when sliced. Seeds can be planted under cloches in March for early harvesting in July. The main crop should be sown between May and July. Sow in drills about 2cm, ¾in deep and thin to a final spacing of 7.5cm, 3in apart. Seeds are actually a cluster so several plants develop from one seed – you will therefore need to thin them out to a single plant when they are about 2.5cm, 1in high. Plants need an even supply of water – too much and they may split, too little and they get woody. In very dry weather water every two weeks. Beetroot takes 60 – 90 days to mature and normal globe shaped beetroots are mature when the size of a cricket ball. One pest that you might encounter when growing beetroot is the flea beetle which attacks the leaves, making holes and preventing you from using the leaves in salads but of course you can feed these to your hens. Otherwise they are usually pest free.

POTATOES AND ONIONS

I usually plant some potatoes and onions even though these are cheap in the shops. Pink Fir Apples are a particularly interesting potato to grow – they look a bit like Jerusalem artichokes – long and knobbly - and are very tasty. Your hens shouldn't be interested in either potato plants or onion sets. The danger is that they may scratch up the onion sets; they may also expose your potatoes by scratching around in the earth after you have earthed up around them so you may have to protect them with a low fence. Potato leaves are poisonous to hens although I've heard of hens eating the leaves to no ill effect.

There are many different varieties of potatoes including early ones to use as new potatoes and maincrop potatoes which are harvested in August. You should obtain seed potatoes in February and chit them. This involves placing them in single layers on trays or in egg boxes in a shed. You should place them rose end up (that is the end with the most eyes from which sprouts are starting to form). The temperature should be between 4°C and 10°C. You should leave the potatoes for about six to eight weeks and they do need light (but not direct sunlight) – leaving them in total darkness would result in them producing long but weak shoots. You should plant your tubers in March or early April. You need to dig holes and allow 5cm, 2in of soil to cover them. You should plant them with shoots uppermost and they should be 23cm, 9in apart in rows 60cm, 2ft apart. You should then earth up the potato plants, once established, in May. This means you create a mound of earth round the plants as this helps protect them from frost and prevents the developing potatoes near the surface from turning green as it excludes the light. There is usually enough moisture in the soil in April and May so you don't need to water at this stage. During dry weather you should water on a weekly basis as potatoes hate water accumulating around their roots. Early potatoes are usually ready for lifting when the plants are in full flower in June/July. Use a fork as a lever to lift the plant and collect the potatoes that have formed at the end of the roots. Maincrop potatoes should be planted in the same way with a little more room between the rows and these are not lifted until the tops have died down, usually in September.

Onions are easiest to grow as sets and planted out in March. A good variety of red onion, Red Baron, is definitely worth growing. The soil should be high in organic matter, preferably with well rotted manure dug into the soil the autumn before. They like free-draining soil and do not do well on heavy clay soil. Otherwise they are easy to grow. Spacing is important - if you space them widely you will get large onions but obviously there will be fewer of them. For medium sized onions space them 5cm, 2in apart in rows about 25cm, 10in apart. You could then thin them out slightly and use some as spring onions in May. Push the onion sets into the soil to half their depth. Look at them every couple of weeks and push any back in that have come right out of the ground. They do not like to be buried but prefer to grow on the surface. Onions require a little watering while the plants establish themselves but after that are best left unwatered. In mid August the tops of your onions will bend over and this stops growth and exposes the bulbs to sunlight so that they can ripen. They will be ready for harvesting in September. Some people say onions should be grown in the same area only one year in three; others that you can grow onions in the same patch every year! Do not grow onions near peas and beans (see page 84).

COURGETTES AND TOMATOES

I usually grow some courgettes and tomatoes in grow bags and my hens stay well clear of these plants – they do not interest them at all. Although my hens do enjoy eating tomatoes, especially the seeds, they don't try and take them off the plants – maybe the leaves, which have such a strong smell, put them off.

I usually grow Gardener's Delight (a popular variety of cherry tomato) and they can be very successful providing we have a long, warm, sunny summer. Outdoor tomatoes are grown from plants and are readily available from garden centres in late spring. Plants can be planted outside once the first flowering truss can be seen and once all risk of frost has passed, usually at the end of May. If using growbags or pots you must keep the tomato plants well watered and it is a good idea to use a bio tomato feed every two weeks. Tomatoes should be ripening up and ready for picking from mid August through September.

Courgettes are relatively easy to grow and do well in grow bags. You can either buy seedlings in May from your local garden centre or grow them from seeds for transplanting once the last frosts have passed. Courgettes need a bed of rich compost and animal manure. They will need regular watering but it is best to water around the plants as watering over the plants may cause the fruits to rot. You will also have to protect against slugs. Plants carry separate male and female flowers. The male stalks are plain while the female bears the fruit. The female flowers must be pollinated for fruit to form - bumble bees usually do this for us - otherwise you can hand pollinate the female flowers by taking the male flower, stripping off the petals and bringing the anthers into contact with the female stigmas. Pick them while still small in August and September and the plants will keep producing more until the cold weather sets in and stops production. You can grow yellow skinned courgettes but their flavour is much the same as the green and you can also grow yellow or green round courgettes which are ideal for stuffing. If you want marrows, just leave the courgettes and they will grow large very quickly. Although courgettes are basically small marrows there are specific courgette varieties that have been bred to bear lots of small fruits instead of a few large marrows. Zucchini F1 is a recognised variety of courgette while Long Green Trailing is a marrow variety.

JERUSALEM ARTICHOKES

Artichokes are incredibly easy to grow. Once you have planted some artichoke tubers you will have an increasing supply of artichokes to enjoy for years to come (the only downside is that the tubers tend to become a little smaller each year). Rather like mint they will grow back every year because you will not manage to dig up every tuber and the ones left in the ground will grow again next spring. Try and plant the tubers on the north side of your patch to avoid shading other crops as the foliage can grow up to 3 metres, 10 feet high. Jerusalem artichoke are a bit like sunflowers in that they grow so tall, but their leaves are smaller and they only actually flower in very hot summers.

Artichokes are grown from tubers which can be purchased from seed suppliers/garden centres or from tubers saved from the year before. They will grow in almost any soil but well-manured clay soils produce the heaviest crops. Tubers should be planted in February about 8cm, 3in deep in the soil and should be at least 30cm, 1ft apart with about 90cm, 3ft between rows. They only need watering if it is very dry in August and this should enhance the yield. Once they have reached their full height their stalks may easily be blown over in the wind but you can cut them to half their height in the autumn without damaging the tubers which should be harvested whenever you require them from November onwards. Your hens will love nibbling at the tubers - chuck them a few when you are digging them up. Jerusalem artichokes also provide a wind break for your hens and a wonderful shady spot when your hens need some respite from the sun in the summer.

PURPLE SPROUTING BROCCOLI AND KALE

Plant some sprouting broccoli seedlings in the early summer and, with any luck, you will have some lovely purple broccoli spears to enjoy the following spring. If you have been growing beans of any sort, plant the broccoli plants in the same patch, when you remove the bean plants. The soil will be full of nitrogen and just right for the broccoli. Purple sprouting broccoli is probably the most popular variety for home growing. It is hardy and produces a succession of small flowerheads for cropping over a long season from winter to late spring, a time when not many other vegetables are in season. You can either grow broccoli from seeds in a propagator or greenhouse or buy plants to plant out in late May. You should leave about 60cm, 2ft between plants and between rows. They do take up a lot of space, grow quite tall and have a long growing season so be warned! In my experience the seedlings tend to grow with slightly crooked stems. You will probably have a problem with caterpillars eating the leaves as the broccoli plants develop. You should pick them off by hand and feed them to your chickens. Do not get too disheartened – the lower leaves tend to shrivel and can be picked off and the broccoli seems to develop successfully despite the caterpillars. The plants tend to be top heavy so you can either earth them up or stake them to prevent them toppling over.

Harvest the heads before they have a chance to flower. If you harvest regularly without stripping each plant completely, the side shoots will keep providing more heads so you should be able to pick broccoli over a period of about eight weeks. Calabrese is grown in the same way but produces a large central flowerhead. Once harvested, the plant will produce smaller sideshoots.

Kale is also useful in providing you with greens in the winter and you can use the young leaves in salads. Your hens will enjoy any surplus kale. Kale does well on ground previously used for a potato crop so you could easily grow some after you have harvested early potatoes in June. Plant seeds outside from April to June in 12mm, ½in drills and you should be able to harvest your kale from November through the winter. Rows should be 30cm, 1ft apart. Nero di Toscana (also known as Black Tuscany or Cavolo Nero) produces an excellent crop and Red Winter produces red frilly leaves on purple stems so is very attractive. Redbor is another red variety for picking through the winter and young leaves can also be used in salads. Hungry Gap is a late variety which you can plant in July for harvesting the following spring. I have tried Pentland Brig which lasted well through the winter, producing green curly-edged leaves. Kale is extremely hardy, withstanding very low temperatures and therefore is not killed off by frosts. You can feed the odd, less than perfect leaves to your hens. Once your kale and broccoli plants are finished with in the late spring, your hens will be very keen to clear up any green leaves that are left and will strip plants down to the woody stalks.

SWEET CORN

I wasn't going to include sweet corn because it takes up quite a lot of space; on the other hand hens absolutely love it. You might like to try growing some and once the plants are established provided you block any way of your hens scratching around the plants, the cobs safely enclosed in their wrappings, will be safe to develop in peace. Sweet corn needs a moisture-retentive, free-draining soil to which well-rotted manure has been added a few weeks before planting. It is probably best to sow seeds in pots under cover in late spring, and then thin to leave the strongest seedlings. Plant them out when the danger of all frosts has passed. It is best to plant seedlings in a block – say 8 plants spaced about 30cm, 1ft apart. The reason for this is that sweet corn is pollinated by wind. The male flowers stand above the top of the plants and shed large amounts of pollen. The female flower is an immature cob with a thin tube hanging from each grain with silk forming at the end. In order for the seeds to develop each strand of silk must receive its own pollen grain. Growing the plants in a block gives them a better chance of pollination.

Growing sweet corn in this country is slightly risky since it needs a long, warm growing season to do well. Keep the soil moist and water well once the plants begin to flower. Plants may need staking as they are shallow rooted – or you could earth up round the plants to make them more stable. Each plant will only produce about two cobs. When they are ready the silks will wither and turn brown. You can peel back the leaves and test for ripeness by pushing your thumb into a grain. If the liquid runs clear it is unripe. If it's milky, then it's ripe and if it is thick, it is over-ripe. Cobs should be eaten as soon after picking as possible because after 24 hours the sugars in the corn start to turn to starch. Your hens will be kept very busy picking the corn out of any surplus cobs!

GROWING HERBS

My herb garden survives pretty much intact as hens won't touch the parsley, rosemary, sage, chives, majoram, thyme, coriander or mint. Although I have read on a forum of someone whose hens do eat the mint in their garden. I grow borage and dill in pots which are not touched. Good King Henry thrives in the garden and surprisingly does not appeal. Lavender lines our steps and path into the garden and is definitely of no interest to the hens. Chickens definitely won't touch fennel. I have read on a forum, though, that some hens are particularly partial to chives, parsley and will also eat spring onions! Here are some easy herbs to grow:

CHIVES

Once you have planted some chives, they will reseed themselves and turn up in various different places in your garden. Chives are useful in the kitchen, are perennial and produce attractive flowers that you can use in salads or to make chive vinegar. My chickens do not eat chives but apparently some people's hens are rather partial to it!

CORIANDER

Coriander grows well in the herb garden and the hens have not eaten the leaves. However I have noticed they like to eat the seeds. Coriander is an attractive annual with a dual purpose because you can use both the leaves and seeds. As soon as the seeds start to ripen in August cut down the plants. The seeds will become more fragrant the longer they are kept and are useful in cooking.

DILL

Dill is an annual but quite difficult to use as it grows very quickly, reaching about 1m, 3ft high, looking a bit like a fennel plant with yellow flowers in umbels. By the time I decide I want to use dill to flavour a sauce it has grown past its best! The seeds can be used but are not as useful as coriander seeds – you can make dill vinegar by steeping the seeds in vinegar for three weeks. The leaves go very well with salmon. My hens don't eat the dill.

MINT

Mint, a perennial, of which there are several kinds, spreads, as I am sure you are aware. You should grow it in a pot if you are worried about the space it will take up. It flowers in July/August and then dies back. The good new is as long as your hens have grass they shouldn't be interested in your mint.

OREGANO (Also known as **WILD MAJORAM**)

The Greeks used this culinary herb, known as 'oros ganos' - joy of the mountain. Oregano (oregano vulgare) is very closely related to sweet majoram (oregano majorana). It is an easy herb to grow and, like mint, spreads and reseeds itself so can pop up in different places in your garden. My hens don't touch the majoram but fresh or dried, it is meant to help prevent chickens getting coccidiosis; some people buy dried oregano and add it to their hens' feed.

PARSLEY

Parsley is biennial. Seeds take quite a while to germinate and prefer warmish soil. Once you have parsley it will last from early summer, well into the autumn and, if you cover the plants will last through the winter and into the next summer. My chickens don't eat the parsley.

ROSEMARY

Like sage, rosemary can become a huge bush and is an evergreen so a useful herb in the winter. Rosemary has lovely blue flowers which bees are attracted to. Again your chickens won't touch rosemary as it has such a pungent smell.

SAGE

Sage is a useful herb to have in your garden and most chickens won't touch it but a small plant can become quite a large bush spread out over a considerable space so if you like sage you will be well-stocked!

SAVORY

Winter savory is the easiest one to have in your garden because it is a perennial. Summer savory is an annual with rather an insignificant flavour and quite difficult to grow. Winter savory is an evergreen with a stronger flavour and useful in the winter when not all herbs are available. Your hens should ignore it and you can use it in any bean dish as it is a traditional companion.

SORREL

I grow broad leaf sorrel. I do have to keep it covered with a Victorian bell cloche as my hens would eat the leaves if they got the chance and have done in the past. The leaves contain oxalic acid which is supposed to be toxic to hens although in small quantities has no ill effect. You can plant seed in the spring and harvest the leaves in the summer for a salad or sorrel soup or use like spinach. Once the plant is established you can divide the roots and replant them. Keep it covered and it will last through the winter.

TARRAGON

French tarragon is the one to grow, rather than the Russian variety but you need to buy it as a plant and transfer to a sunny spot in your herb garden – it prefers well drained soil which is not too rich. You can take cuttings or propagate by the division of the roots later on to give you more plants. Tarragon is a perennial and can grow quite tall – it is meant to be an evergreen but usually does shed its leaves. It is a shrub-like plant with woody main stems, tender, narrow leaves and a strong smell. The leaves go well with chicken or fish or can be used to make tarragon vinegar. Your hens shouldn't touch it as the leaves are quite aromatic.

THYME

Your chickens shouldn't eat thyme, the exception being that if thyme is the only greenery around and there is no grass, then they might well tuck in. There are lots of different varieties – lemon thyme is particularly good. The plants are shrubby, decorative evergreens growing to about 30cm, 12in high. Plants tend to straggle. Lemon thyme does not seed so plants need to be replaced every three years.

LIFE ON A SMALLHOLDING
IN THE 1930S AND 40S

BY
MAY WEDDERBURN CANNAN

*My great aunt, May Wedderburn Cannan, was a first world war poet
– she wrote an autobiography, Grey Ghosts and Voices about her life
before and during the First World War. The sequel remains unpublished
and tells her story before, during and after the Second World War. She
built up a successful smallholding in Staffordshire which she was forced
to abandon during the war but returned to afterwards. May had married
Percival Slater, after the first war, whom she refers to as PJ – he
returns to the army during the war, as a major commanding a Searchlight
Battery and is promoted to Brigadier by the end of the war.*

*Here are some extracts from her unpublished sequel in which May
describes the ups and downs of life on her smallholding with her poultry,
sheep and later pigs:*

We moved, in October 1934, into the country; twelve miles
West of Wolverhampton just inside the Staffordshire border,
we had found, quite by chance, our dream house. It was small,
old and whitewashed and had been an Agricultural Holding.
Its attic windows looked West over Wrekin and the Shropshire
Clees and East over the damson orchard; and when I first
saw it, there was bracken and hare-bells in the rough cart
track which led from the lane to its little drive. We treated it
gently and with great care, and when we had added eight feet
to the length of its kitchen and put a bathroom above and
given it a new kitchen behind the small narrow parlour that

looked south west across the lawn and added a bedroom over that, it sighed gently and accepted us. It is the house, of all the houses we had, that I still think of as 'Home'. It had six acres.

The Home Meadow which ran down, with a wonderful hedge of hollies where afterwards our sheep lay up in shelter from the westerly gales to the Middle Meadow; and beyond to the Far Meadow whose gate opened on to Green Lane. On the right was the orchard with its run of old stone wall and a two-storied dovecot and from it ran down alongside Middle and Far Meadows, the Clover Patch which had once been sown to clover and in front, to the left of the house, lay a south-sloping acre of kitchen garden and directly under the house windows a small lawn and two rose beds. The drive had a hedge of damsons and in front of them down its entire length I planted the first and most beautiful of all my herbaceous borders. There was a large, dark stone-build stable which became a store and above a loft which turned into a workshop and held two workbenches and a coke stove; and a small wooden stable with two loose boxes where Donkey lived and was joined later by Cherry, the chestnut pony and an old shed which housed by an inch or so my Rattletrap ...

It was two miles to the village which had one shop and a Post Office which was our nearest pillar box: it was 600 feet above sea level and we were told that, come winter, we should probably be snowed up. The charming old people who had owned it had not been able to do much in their last years and the fields were empty and the garden was full of weeds. There were a great many enormous rats which PJ shot, while he shaved, with his Service Revolver, through the bathroom window as they ran across the yard. The wind blew and it was very cold. A stray cat who became known as Kitty-Cat came to live with us making friends with the dogs and lying with them in front of the library fire and it was the most wonderful place in the world. One either has a feeling for Land or one has not. We had. I bought coal and peat and sawed wood for our fires – ordered straw and hay and bran and chaff and middlings and wheat and oats. Then I bought a hen house on wheels and from the Snowden brothers 24 Light Sussex hens and a cock. Hatched and reared as free rangers on the wide Yorkshire dales they were perfect for our high windy fields and in the winter laid a wonderful number of brown tinted eggs and in the spring when they went broody were the perfect Mothers for chicks and ducks and geese.

When they were installed and settled down, I bought, since PJ had made and cemented a duck pond, a duck house and went to an auction in the village and found a friend to bid for me for 25 Khaki Campbells. I had no idea when they were knocked down to me that I should have to remove them directly the auction was over; my car had only talc windows at the back and mercifully a roof; the front and sides were wide open. However, I kept a poker face, thanked the friend who helped me carry down the astonished ducks and pile them into the back of the car, stepped on the gas and drove hell for leather for home.

As I got to the gate they began to fly around my head and as I drove into the Home Meadow the first two flew from the windows. There was pandemonium but we were home and dry ...

We made hay that year. We made hay while our hands blistered and our heads ached ... Then we picked our damsons ... what we picked sold well and by that time we had found an experienced ex-service gardener with a lame foot who knew everything and became a valued friend, who could come for two days a week and two smallholding friends who were generous with both help and advice. One of them had, like us, six acres down in the valley; like me he kept hens for egg production (that was my chief plan for the future) and I discovered to keep down the grass for the hens and as his other line he had sheep. At breakfast I said, "Could we keep sheep?"

"Do you," PJ asked coming out from the library with his brief case, "Know enough about sheep?"

"No," I said "But Mr Brazier does and I could learn. He has six acres and keeps six sheep. You run a sheep to an acre ...

I had spent the first ten years of my married life writing. I had written five books and no one had wanted any of them except one ... I had always had a job of work – I believed in work – and now we had all this land. Land was meant to be used and served. It was the fundamental thing. [*and so May got her sheep*] On winter mornings in freezing fog ... I could hear them at the field-yard gate. "Baa" they said. Blackberry with a deep voice and Meadowsweet with her light one ... and I'd push through the warm, soft bodies to the feeding troughs lying under the shelter of the hollies. Then back for the hay for their hay rack – and later on another journey for the roots and a bucket of water ... after that there were the hens and the ducks and the geese. We had three geese and a gander whom I had driven over from a nearby holding, his feet tied, illegally, if loosely in a sack sitting on the seat beside me with my arm round him and his face a good deal nearer mine than I liked, and me driving with one hand and praying we shouldn't meet the village police.

We had got a second hen house and 50 hens by now and I would put the kettles on in the kitchen as I came through and when I got back they'd be boiling and I'd fill and refill the big mixing bowl, measuring the meals according to what they said in those very excellent pamphlets that were published by the Ministry of Agriculture and Fish – they didn't have swill at all – and stir and deal it out into the flatish enamel dishes, one to each six hens. Fifty head of poultry – we had 250 in the end – all in full winter plumage with their black collars round their necks and their silver legs – I just would NOT have yellow legs – were a pretty sight feeding in the early morning sun …. It was lonely sometimes and it was hard work, but it was, I knew even in the very early days, the good life. …

PJ threw himself into his legal work [*he was a solicitor*] …. I threw myself into the farm and village life.

We had 22 lambs that spring and I could call myself a shepherd, albeit an inexperienced one; and out under the sunny orchard wall were 10 broodies waiting to hatch out chicks and presently there were 10 families of hens and chicks in the excellent coops and runs I found and PJ had copied for me during the winter months. From them we ran on a flock of 250 laying hens and I raised from the same reliable Sussex hens 50 ducks and 25 geese.

I also had a side line (from the best of the cockerels among my hatchings) of Stock Cockerels for breeding, for which I could ask £2 a head. They had their own quarters down in the Clover Patch.

My real worry was the marketing. I had a contract with a small multiple firm of two shops in Wolverhampton for a regular delivery of eggs twice a week and never fell below the agreed quota or sold an egg that was more than three or four days old. The eggs were delivered by me and included an agreed number of duck eggs. Though the shop manager was far from friendly all went well for a time and then suddenly, and it was market day, he refused the duck eggs, just saying he did not want them. I pointed out that they were included in the contract and we stood and looked at each other over the boxes for some moments, in an angry silence. In the end I won but he was so appallingly rude that I gave notice as it had been agreed I could, to terminate the contract at the end of the next week.

I found and signed a contract with another shop and went back the following week to collect my egg boxes. Being told that they had not got them I asked for their cost and sticking it out, they were eventually literally thrown at me over the counter. As I left, the shop owner came in and asked me to re-consider my decision. He had never, he said, had a bad egg from me not like those Higglers who would slip in a few that already smelt to high heaven. I said this was impossible but I would tell him the reason for the trouble. I had overheard, waiting for my boxes, a conversation between his Manager and one of his staff. He considered the bargain with me had been made over his head and had been determined to wreck it from the start. It was the beginning of my rather low opinion of shopkeepers ... Most people are good farmers and bad buyers and sellers or the other way round. I was certainly a bad seller. The Farmer's Weekly never in its tables of prices, seemed to give those for my area; the shops tried endlessly to beat me down; and if I left them I laid myself open to criticism among my fellow producers (especially the Higglers) of underselling them. I grew to dread Wednesdays and Fridays, the days I took my eggs in and dreamed about it in my sleep. When the Packing Stations began and I was forced to sell to them I was thankful because at least the prices were fixed and I had no more bargaining to do. But there were in some ways a disaster. The eggs were collected only once a week and I found out later what I was not supposed to know, that my boxes were often not even opened for a fortnight and the eggs might not be sold for another week depending on where they might be sent to make up a quota. It seemed a shame. Beautiful fresh eggs gone over and all because of greed on the part of the shop – the middle men!

I became more skilful in the garden learning from our three day a week man and reading a great deal, and presently I was marketing raspberries which are easily picked, weighed and packed and some strawberries. I tried French artichokes but no one in Wolverhampton, I was told, knew what to do with them and they were useless though they were selling at 2/6 a head in London. I tried early lettuce and sold 300 one week at a halfpenny each; next week they were a farthing and the week after they were being thrown away in the Bridgenorth market – there was a glut. I gave that one up and tried cut flowers, growing only the tidy, long lasting ones like scabious and pyretheums, and gypsophila which always sold because of wreaths. It was no use to compete with daffodils – we were too late in the year – and presently when the Worcester apples, of which we had planted a small orchard at the end of the garden, were fruiting, we sold these ...

We were not very well off. Provincial Solicitors did not make all that much and my father-in-law would not expand. The business men we knew made far more than us – not that I wanted to make what they made or to live, or be, like them – and what I made with the farm came in very handy. It became a way of life, and I came, very dearly to love the land. I read about it, listened to my farming neighbours and thought much. My Bible at that time was A G Street's *Land Everlasting* and my love was our six acres – acres, dear acres, of toil. Of course there was the lighter side. There was the Annual Village Show which was quite big and attracted well over 1,000 visitors and in which I showed eggs and herbaceous flowers. To my delight and astonished surprise I got a 1st for eggs and a 2nd for flowers – beaten by a professional who had more land and more skill. The first time, my eggs carefully unwashed and carefully handled were laid out on green leaves in a bowl; the local Higgler materialised at my side. "That's a nice lot," she said and picked one up turning it over and over in her hand. I was very green and said nothing. "Don't" whispered an urgent voice on my other side, "let her do that, she's rubbing off the bloom." I just hadn't known …

[And then in 1938 when war seemed likely PJ went back into the army, having been offered a Searchlight Battery, part of the Royal Artillery of the TA. May wrote to Farmers' Weekly:]

'Sir, four years ago I bought a small farm. I reclaimed the pasture which was in a bad way, limed, slagged, repaired hedges, planted vegetables, roots and young fruit trees and stocked it with poultry and sheep. I have not had any guidance from the Ministry of Agriculture as to what would be wanted of me and my land in the event of war.

In the last war a vacillating policy was pursued. The Government urged all producers to increase their stock and 'Egg and Poultry Demonstration' trains were run through England to encourage them to do so. In May 1917 an alarmist article by an Agricultural Professor – *The Hen is Eating Your Food'* was followed by a drastic cutting down of stocks and in 1918 there was a severe shortage.

I am aware that my Holding is small; a mere drop in the ocean; but in this village there are four others in the same position, and there must be hundreds elsewhere.

Could not the Ministry do two things:

1. Make a definite statement as to what will be wanted of small farmers and their land in time of war. It is useless to spend money and labour running a mixed farm and raising stock if the Ministry's policy is to cut down the stock, grub up our hedges, and plough us into the nearest large farm.

2. Bring back into being and enlist now, volunteers for the Women's Land Army of the last war; volunteers being given, if not a uniform at least a badge to wear. There are hundreds of girls passing out yearly from agricultural colleges who because there is no Land Army will take service in other organisations ...'

They printed my letter in the magazine and presently I saw in the National Press that the Ministry were setting up Shadow County Committees to deal with a possible Land Army ... [*May sat on one of the committees and did her bit to help recruit Land girls and 1939 came*]

The Farm flourished, but I was anxious knowing that wars started after Harvest time and rang up my usual supplier and ordered enough poultry meal and grain to see me through. My man thought I was mad. "The price will go down, he told me, after harvest; you shouldn't order now."

"It won't go down," I said, "It will go up – there will be a war."

He had not, he said, heard of any war, and only after some persuasion agreed to take my cheque and deliver what I ordered. That was in July .... [*The war started*] ...

Then the first blow fell. Though food rationing didn't begin till January people had begun to hoard and wouldn't use sugar and there was no sale for the damson crop. The fruit rotted ... Three ships came into the Mersey with animal feeding stuffs and were turned back by Chamberlain's orders on the score we couldn't afford it and that winter hard-bitten farmers up in the North stayed in their houses because they could not face the cattle in the yards crying for food; and poultry keepers bought packets of cream crackers for their flocks at $8\frac{1}{2}$d a pound – and I thanked God that I had bought what I had bought …..

That January 1940 it was very cold. With the first snowfall Jim [*May's son*] fell ill and the Doctor, getting over just in time, diagnosed scarlet fever. Well, he couldn't be moved, the roads were already becoming blocked. He would report it but it was I who must cope – which was what I wanted. Later that night the blizzard came. Letting the dogs out at 10pm I saw how it would be, persuaded Jo-Jo [*May's new, wonderful assistant who was a trained gardener*] to go to bed and when she was safely asleep, took my lantern and went out again. Putting it down on the snow and praying the ARP would not see I began to dig. The snow was not only coming down it was blowing in sheets off the higher fields to the East. I dug and dug, making with a four foot wall, a corral as a shelter for the sheep. We had got them all up into the Home Meadow, nearest the house and with the shelter, to the West, of the Hollies; and our ten hen houses were all up in the top meadows for the winter too.

It was frightening digging, with all that snow coming inexorably down, alone in the dark, but the sheep heard me and came, baaing softly, and presently my wall was high enough and I fetched straw and spread it and called them in. They trusted me, came in, began to settle, lay down, and I went in to bed ..

I was woken by Jo-Jo tapping at my door. "It's snowed and everything's under. I can't see the gates." I dressed hurriedly and went down. We fed the dogs and cats and breakfasted. Jim was marvellous saying he'd be all right and should he have the dogs? He'd hear the news and tell us later what it was. I had brought in two spades and we dug ourselves out of the kitchen door. The snow was up round the windows and the house seemed very dark. We dug a trench across the yard to the garage where the mangolds were stored; then a trench – the snow was over six feet deep – to the corral wide enough for one to pass with a bucket in either hand and fed the sheep. They were all there and safe except that Bramble was frozen by her wet fleece to the ground and could not get up. I fetched the shears and cut her loose. Mercifully they were all used to my handling them and no one panicked ... Down in the valley where my neighbour-farmer had a flock of 200 they did not come up for their feed and when he sent his dog for them she came back without them. He found them huddled under the hedges, frozen not only to the ground but to each other so that when one tried to get up she was held down by the weight of the rest. He and his men had a dreadful time freeing them. They could not of course be used to being handled as our 12 were. We stopped for a quick lunch and at 4pm that afternoon we dug our way to the last hen house and fed the hungry birds ...

And then it froze. The water froze in the pipe that led from the bore hole chamber where it was pumped with the electric motor and there was no water except what we pumped by hand and carried up from the cottage in the field below where mercifully there was enough for them to let us have some. And then it froze in the houses ... Next the electricity failed. Well, we had lamps and oil and a store of candles; and there was the kitchen range. What was left was the telephone so that though the Doctor could not reach us I could report and get instructions. On the morning of the fourth day Mr Brazier, my partner in sheep, appeared coming across the fields with a sack on his back, a shepherd's crook in one hand

and a can of milk in the other. He had not , he said, been able to sleep, thinking of us. He had brought us four loaves, some cheese and a chicken his wife had cooked. He warned me not to try the road as it was chock full and I should drown in the drifts. The safest way was over the higher fields by which he had come, but to take a long stick and be careful.

For five weeks nothing on wheels could get to us. When we had finished the afternoon feeds one of us took my rucksack and went down and collected the food they brought out and left stacked for us at the bottom of the lane, bringing what I had asked for on the phone. No one in the farms or the village had time to give any more help, they were all hard pressed.

Then one night, over the field I saw a light and went to investigate. The electricity board had come to repair the grid. It was bitter cold and I said when they had finished to come in and get warm and made coffee and sandwiches - one of them had been in the TA. And after that we had light and the fires and cooker but still no water; the pipe from the water pump to the house still being frozen. I got out the garden hose, plugged it onto the tap from which we filled the duck pond, in the pump chamber, dragged it across the yard and up a ladder and fed it under the eaves into the tank in our small attic and we had water again for washing and for the stock … and Jim was better and presently the Doctor would be able to come …

I came up from collecting the shopping, unloaded the rucksack and sat down on the stairs and suddenly I couldn't walk – and there Jo-Jo found me, helped me to bed, said she would put a tray for Jim outside his door – I had refused to let her go in and catch the fever – and I slept the clock round and woke recovered. It was only exhaustion …

118

When the thaw came the cellar flooded and going down for eggs from the crock I stepped into four feet of water. Bottled fruit, jam, eggs and our small store of beer and wine were all under and as I looked empty jars from the higher shelf floated off, filled and sank with a gurgling sound. Remembering a boys' book of adventure I fetched chalk, marked the water level on the wall, told no one and went to bed. Next morning the water was no higher. I tried siphoning but couldn't manage it … in the end it seeped away, leaving horrible mud …It was the time that became known as the "Phoney War".

Meanwhile, what I suppose I had always known would happen, happened and we were told to reduce our stock to a figure that would make my egg production and poultry farming completely uneconomic.

Fruit was unsaleable since sugar rationing had begun and taking the sheep down now that the thaw had come to the lower pasture in the village, Mr Brazier told me he would no longer be able to keep them. "The bottom" he said, "is out of that market – ploughing up everything, that's the plan. No place for smallholdings." He would take a job at one of the big farms - and he would be, I knew, only too welcome …

Sitting by myself over the embers of the carefully raked up fire that night I tried to look at it objectively. What I could make by myself would be negligible … it wouldn't work out. Before the end of the great freeze, I had buried, using a pick to get through the hard, unyielding earth, our beloved cocker spaniel. She was old and had been failing all that long, hard winter and when at last the vet could get up to see her it was cancer of the throat and all I could do for her was to give her merciful sleep … Bramble and some of the others had lambed before I took them down to the valley and I hadn't lost a lamb and now I knew that they, who had followed me so trustfully down the lane would presently be sold into alien hands. I had gone ahead and called them - I never drove them - and led by Meadowsweet, they had followed me - and I had betrayed them ... It was all gone what we had built up with so much hope and toil and loving care ...

I wrote to PJ and a day or two later got the answer ... "There is no use making a misery of this war. It is a shame that all our efforts to produce a food unit that might be useful in war have come to nothing; stock reduced and everything unwanted but at least you have improved the fields if they are to be ploughed and I have been coming round to thinking it might be better if you became a rolling stone and followed my fortunes if I am not to go abroad.... *[So Jo-Jo joined the Wrens and May found a tenant and from April 1940 for the next five years she moved from place to place during the war to be near her husband's battery. In April 1945 they return to the farm:* ... The drive was covered in weeds. The herbaceous bed that ran its length and had been my pride and joy had gone under – brambles and nettles and ground elder. There was no flutter of wings by the pigeon house ... There were store cattle in the meadows. The kitchen garden seemed a ruin – gone under save for a few depressed looking cabbages and the bare arms of sprouts. The Worcesters we had planted at the far end, a small orchard, had grown tall ... But we were home. The old dog knew it ... We made a tour of our fields. When we changed tenants half way through the war the new ones had not wanted the land and it had been handed over to the local War Agriculture Committee. They had let it to a smallholder to whom the store cattle, and presently we found two horses who were turned out to graze at the end of their day, belonged.

One duck house was missing. They had not wanted the ducks and had broken up the house for firewood. The other house was empty. Half a dozen sad looking Rhode Islands stood around a shabby looking hen house that hadn't seen a brush of creosote for five years. The others seemed derelict.

The cattle stampeded whenever we approached them. It must have been they who had torn up and trampled the tall wire fencing for the Stock Cockerel Houses in the Clover Patch. Half of it was underground, grass and weeds growing up through what remained of the mesh – the other half stood up in the air, like wire in No Man's Land ....

I began work in the kitchen garden – we'd have a row of early peas ... I wrote to the greatest duck breeder in the fens at Ixworthy. "I can't afford your lovely white Campbells now but if you could, and it isn't too small an order, let me have five Khaki Campbell ducks and a drake of a good laying strain I'd be most grateful" – The answer came, the ducks were on their way ....

I cleaned, mended and creosoted their house and PJ scythed some bracken for litter - it saved a little money for straw – did the same for the Rhode Islands and bought another house for the 24 Light Sussexes I had ordered from free range breeders in Yorkshire and felt that we were in business again.

… It was uphill work on the holding. There was no money, now, I was told, in sheep; pigs were the thing. With the first

profit made from the hens I bought a sow, called her Susan, a Wessex Saddleback and when she had her first farrow she produced 12 piglets and we sold them at 10 weeks at £6 a piece – with her second farrow I bought another sow – Serena – and presently there were eight up in the far meadows free ranging and living in little ark-type houses as tame as could be and only too anxious to follow me about like dogs …

I went on working. Knowing better from pre-war days than to try veg. I specialised in raspberries; easy to pick and pack; strawberries; backbreaking work but it paid; and the hard fruits from the orchard and fields: damsons, apples and pears. The cut flowers did well ... The eggs were collected once a fortnight by the Egg Marketing Board and though I hated to see my beautiful fresh eggs left to grow stale – and gathered from the girl who drove the van, inadvertently that often the boxes weren't even opened for another fortnight at least it saved me the old nightmare of bargaining with the rapacious shops. ...rationing went on ... we had it for another ten years, it ended in 1956 ... at the lowest we had 2 ounces of butter and tea a week, an ounce of cheese, 2 ounces of margarine or cooking fat; one half jar of jam or marmalade a month, and about one egg in 14 days of three weeks owing to the insane slaughter of hens at the beginning of the war to save feeding stuffs....

We were told to grow sunflowers for the hens and I grew a great line of them in the kitchen garden and had fun rubbing the ripe seeds from the flower heads that are like honeycombs but the hens would not eat them. They were worse, they said, than the oats which the Government made me feed them instead of good wheat ...

And then I got a call from the local representative of the War Agricultural Committee [*he had come to assess the Holding, now that their lease to our late tenants had run out. If the Holding was marked A it reverted wholly to May and PJ, if B they can keep supervisory control, if C it remains under them*] ... I made that man come round and look at every single thing – at the mended gates and fences; at the refurbished and new hen and duck houses, at the pig arks up the meadows; at the breeding sows with their piglets, at the 250 in-lay hens and the 50 ducks; at the geese and the gander and 23 goslings; at the two milking goats and their growing kids; at the white washed damson trees in the orchard; the pruned apples and pears and soft fruit in the kitchen garden; at the orderly rows of peas and beans and cabbage and spinach beet; at the potatoes and the roots that we grew for the stock; at the lines of cut flowers.

"And now," I said, as we reached the drive gate in the gathering dusk, "what are you going to do?"

"Well," he said soothingly, "after all that, I confess I cannot see my way to assess you at less than 'A'.

"I should hope so," I said – very inadvisably for he might have changed his mind. "You took my land when it was in good heart and when it was in your care you let it relapse into ruin," …

It seemed sometimes a desperate business. It was always a worrying, a tiring business but it was a way of life and a way of life worth living. The Holding little by little season by season had got on to its feet again.

My philosophy was that I gave the beasts, who were my friends, a happy life while they were with me – freedom, kindness, shelter, as good food as I could get and when the day came, as quick and unfrightening a death as was possible – as much as that one can sometimes not give to one's children … bar the cockerels which were sold for breeding and no one was going to pay two pounds for a bird and then ill treat it, I never sold a bird alive off the place knowing what can happen in the backs of some retail shops and I knew where the pigs went … Hens in batteries, and deep litter sheds! Calves and, may God forgive us, them and the lambs who are threatened next, in pens so small they cannot turn round in them and never see the sun! Poultry farming! I would never stand for it. It is cruel, wicked and in the end disastrous for the land and it is possible with hard work, and I mean hard work and without the greed for money to make a modest living ...

Index